John Mackinnon Robertson

Patriotism and Empire

John Mackinnon Robertson

Patriotism and Empire

ISBN/EAN: 9783337165246

Printed in Europe, USA, Canada, Australia, Japan

Cover: Foto ©Suzi / pixelio.de

More available books at **www.hansebooks.com**

Patriotism and Empire

BY
JOHN M. ROBERTSON
AUTHOR OF
'THE SAXON AND THE CELT,' ETC.

London
Grant Richards
1899

To

MONCURE DANIEL CONWAY,

WHO HAS WROUGHT FOR PEACE, TRUTH, JUSTICE

AND INTERNATIONAL RIGHTEOUSNESS

IN BOTH HEMISPHERES

DURING TWO GENERATIONS,

THESE PAGES ARE DEDICATED

WITH AFFECTION AND ESTEEM.

CONTENTS

PART I
	PAGE
THE SPRINGS OF PATRIOTISM AND MILITARISM	1

PART II
THE MILITARIST REGIMEN	71

PART III
THE THEORY AND PRACTICE OF IMPERIALISM	138
ADDENDA	205
INDEX	206

Patriotism and Empire

PART I

The Springs of Patriotism and Militarism

I

HISTORY and poetry, we may be sure, will not willingly let die the antique tale of the three hundred who at Thermopylæ held out for Sparta against the Persian host, knowing that there could be but one end, and facing it with a stern exaltation, combing their long hair for that, the last festival, and singing the while—

'Singing of death and of honour that cannot die.'

It is true, there are offsets. There was no military wisdom in defending the pass after the Persians had got behind it; and if it was to be defended, it should have been, as before, from the narrows, not, as was finally done, by way of a sortie. Between the tactics of Leonidas below and those of the Phocians above, we are moved to say with Sir George Cox that 'the generalship, if the story be true, is little better than that of savages.' Nor are the three hundred entitled to all the honours of the fight, as fight, since there fought with them seven hundred Thespians as brave as they, and at least a thousand unconsidered helots, who did their part like men. Nay, the good Herodotus tells twice over that in all four thousand men were slain on the Greek side at Thermopylæ, a statement which Bishop Thirlwall gingerly accepts, and Mr. Grote somewhat perturbedly seeks to explain away. Then there were the Thebans, of whom many were spared, as the story goes, on their asking quarter. With four or five thousand men, to say nothing of the thousands he had sent home, Leonidas might have held the pass up to starvation-point. On the whole, we must suspect, with Sir George Cox, that the facts of the case have not come down to us intact. And when all is said, we know that in every age and stage of human things, from the nameless wars of savages to the most consummately controlled campaigns of so-called civilization, troops of men have died as hardily as those commanded by Leonidas. Yet withal it is a brave tale, and fit to typify an ideal.

Let it be freely agreed that when we come to deal with men bearing themselves bravely under the supreme test of conduct, the open facing of death, whatever was to be said of their action in bringing the crisis about, censure is silenced. This or that war may have been precipitated by arrogance or avarice, obstinacy in injustice or insolent folly, but when those on either side voluntarily put their lives to the stake of the struggle, and the die is thrown, we have passed from the region of debate to that of contemplation, as fellow-creatures looking on destiny and the eternal vicissitude of things. So there will always be for every man, at least 'while *this* machine is to him,' an irreducible thrill before the spectacle of free men going with a high heart to their doom. It is the certainty of that thrill of feeling that gives unchanging force to such words as 'heroism.' There could not be a more telling or a more typical exploitation of our sensations in these matters than is accomplished by M. Rostand in his heroic comedy of 'Cyrano de Bergerac,' which, with its audaciously new versification, its energetic unrealism, and its magnificent management of the *panache* in general, has lately won in France even such a success as was its due in a nation so persistently martial that it takes its sentimentalism almost

4   Patriotism and Empire

solely in the form of fanfaronade. In a superbly preposterous scene, M. Rostand presents to us a corps of the half-starved French besiegers, themselves besieged, of a town held by the Spanish in Flanders. To them comes, in the rapture of her love for the author of the letters she has been receiving daily as from her lover, the beautiful Roxane, in her coach, crammed with provisions, the chivalrous Spaniards having everywhere let it pass their lines on her assurance that she was going to see her lover. Such is war, on the stage.

Just then, as it happens, the corps in question, including both of Roxane's lovers, are awaiting an assault in force which is pretty sure to annihilate them, as it is to fall solely on their trenches. So the starved Gascon cadets hilariously eat and drink like schoolboys at play; and then the fighting begins, and the known lover is brought in dead, killed by the first shot; and as the outworks are surmounted by a host of Spaniards, astonished at the resistance, and asking, 'Who are these men who thus fight to the death?' the superb Cyrano and his band leap forward on the pikes, trolling their song, 'Ce sont les cadets de Gascogne!' So skilful is it all that, even in reading, our smile at the fanfaronade is blended with a swelling in the throat, and we may guess how it touches hot heads and hot hearts in France. To them it all stands for the love of country, for the great name of France, for undying patriotism, as well as for the pride of courage. That is the end of the matter, even as with the tale of the three hundred at Thermopylæ. The moral is that they died 'for Sparta and her laws.' The thrill of sympathy with haughty courage is carried to the account of a certain assumed political virtue; and the habit of mind represented by this assumption gets all the sanction of that strong and pure emotion. It seems clear that 'patriotism,' whatsoever the name may cover, must be the purest of impulses because it is thus allied with the purest of sympathetic feelings. Such is the profound fallacy that it behoves us to disentangle, in the light at once of the antecedents and the consequences of what commonly passes for 'patriotism.'

II

Go back as far as we will in history, by way either of records or of inference from what survives of the primitive, we find groups of people united by what a recent sociologist calls 'consciousness of kind,' and in virtue of

6 Patriotism and Empire

that consciousness prepared to fight with other groups. The two tendencies, the cohesion and the repulsion, are strictly correlative; each involves the other. No law of human progression can well seem more sinister than this primal interdependence of love and hate, of good and evil, of union and destruction; and we shall do well to face the fact in all its grimness at the outset of our questioning. It was assuredly in no 'social compact' for mere neighbourly reciprocity that those early societies were rooted which have evolved into great civilizations. Some marginal communities there may be which wage no wars, having enough ado to fight inclement Nature, and which are held together by the mutual good-will born of continuous collective need, the stragglers being bound to perish; but in the average early tribe a main part of the force of cohesion was the spontaneous hostility to other tribes.

Primus in orbe, let us say, adapting the disputed maxim concerning the making of Gods, *societates fecit timor*—fear first of alien animals, it may be, and later of alien men; but the fear implied the hostile impulse all round; and the men of a society best knew that they loved each other by dwelling on their joint enmity to other societies. And the worst of

Patriotism and Militarism

the fatality was that as societies developed through the ages by way of survival of the fittest, and the primitive gregarious instinct, which is so sufficient in the primitive stage, was gradually weakened by the individual egoism which flourishes on the growth of property, that old love-in-hate, or brotherhood in warfare, became more and more palpably the ruling and enduring force of union, the main representative of the spirit of attraction, and so inevitably took to itself all the sanctions that the instincts of union had ever possessed. The sense of passionate community of feeling is too grateful not to be long cherished in the last form in which individualistic disintegration leaves it possible to an entire community; a community must be disintegrated indeed when, hardened in the perpetual hostilities of the normal competitive and progressive civilization, and lacking any higher ideal of brotherhood, it ceases even to relish the sympathy and synergy that accrue to the state of international war. In our own day we see the society in which commercial competition is perhaps carried furthest, responding with ecstasy to the appeal of 'patriotism' under the form of a war of aggression on an ill-conducted neighbour. The commercial egoist, bent throughout life on besting all rivals, is seen to find a peculiar joy in the chance of an impassioned co-operation in the name of the common good. He whose life's task has been to create burdensome tariffs in his own favour, to undersell and ruin his competitors, to keep down his workmen's wages to enrich himself, is found offering to equip at his own expense a regiment of soldiers, as the expression of his new-found delight in the notion of fellowship. But it takes the old brute instinct of battle, of hate, to work the change, and they who think that, with that instinct asleep again, he will continue zealous to promote the common weal in normal life, are extravagantly astray.

III

Lest this should seem a perversely hard saying, let us see for ourselves how the spirit called patriotism has always correlated with the forces of civic life. In the stormy generations in which we find Roman history taking something like clear shape among the receding mists of legend, we find on one and the same scene the play of an egoism which shrinks from no extremes of tyranny within the society itself, and a vigour of patriotism which shirks no effort for the maintenance of the State against others.

'Then none was for a party,
Then all were for the State.'

So the great rhetorician makes his early Roman sing, confessing the stress of faction already in the days of the decemvirs. But if the song were true, it could only be in the sense that earlier egoism was not scientific enough to use the machinery of faction; for the sense in which 'all were for the State,' as the learned rhetorician incidentally makes known, was one consistent with a constant readiness on the part of each well-to-do citizen to enslave his poorer neighbours for debt. We see the poor farmer going loyally to the war, along with or under his richer neighbour, helping him to defeat the traditional enemy, and returning to be cast in bondage for the debt he has been forced to incur after a previous campaign—forced, that is, by reason of the fact that his farming went to ruin in his absence, while the rich man's farm was tilled by his slaves and managed by his bailiffs. No enemy could have used the poor farmer worse; but the last thing he ever thought of—the one thing he never thought of—was to make common cause with his similarly mishandled congener in the rival State against the creditor class who beggared both alike. That grotesque acquiescence in a partnership from which the poor man derived only the passing gratification of a subterrational passion, while the rich man got that and his riches as well, is a sufficient proof of the strength of the habitual hallucination. The *nexus* could indeed resent his enslavement by his fellow-patriot; but nothing could alter his preconception of the sacredness of patriotism—that is, of the temper of enmity till death towards the whole of the other group, who at worst would but enslave him as a penalty for fighting against them, and who had never made any pretence of being his brothers. Such are the psychological roots of the moral phenomenon we are considering.

It does not concern us here to ask how the Roman community as a whole drifted out of that astonishing state of things into one of less obviously unstable equilibrium : suffice it that this practical definition of patriotism, as mere negative community of malice, involving only the necessary minimum of further co-operation or fellow-feeling, is the burden of all history. The 'three hundred' at Thermopylæ, as we have incidentally seen, had no vestige of any sentiment of normal fellowship with either their helots or their subaltern farmer class, who abroad fought shoulder to shoulder with them against the hereditary foe, only to return to subordination and grinding slavery at home, if any return there were. Helots who might at

Patriotism and Militarism 11

any moment be treacherously massacred by their brutal masters, on the score that they were dangerously healthy and numerous, could nearly always be relied on to fight valiantly against some other set of slave-owners in their own owners' interest. No sense of normal wrong could quicken their intelligence to the point of casting off the insane spell of the ancient 'consciousness of kind.'

IV

But the hapless helots of Sparta and the doomed yeomen of ancient Rome, we shall be told, stood only for the patriotism of unintelligence; and there is a patriotism which is intelligent. Let it merely be noted, then, thus far, how absolutely devoid of all true or constructive fellow-feeling on the part of the aristocratic or ruling class was that concurrence of passion which *they* regarded as patriotism; and how readily the passion broke out between faction and faction at home, as soon as the cessation of fear of invasion from without removed the primary combining pressure. The question now is, when and how and where the alleged purification or rationalization of patriotism began.

It would be tedious to disprove what few

instructed people would affirm, that in medieval Europe matters went very much otherwise than they did in Sparta and Rome; or that even in Athens the spirit of patriotism normally rose above a partnership in domination over tribute-paying allies and a chronic sinking of domestic hates in a more unreasoning hate towards some other community. To that partnership, indeed, Pericles gave a constructive air by his special policy; but that policy itself had its bitter domestic enemies; and it is impossible to show that it furthered fraternity in fostering art and the pride of art and power. The best case framable, perhaps, for a worthy patriotism in past times, would be one drawn up from the history of the Swiss cantons; and that pleading must perforce ignore the phase of mercenary aggression, and dwell solely on the defensive side of Swiss warfare. And, after all, it would give little foothold to those who make much of patriotism as a virtue in empires, where the plea of necessary defence, however customary, is derisory. If it is ever to be shown that patriotism, while preserving the primary character of a union in enmity, has taken on the seemlier spirit of rational and normal sympathy, the proof must be forthcoming from modern politics, and, to be satisfactory, must be in part producible from our

Patriotism and Militarism 13

own affairs. The unwariest sentimentalist will not now go back to the English patriotism of the day of Henry V., whose unification of his people in the conquest of France was so promptly and duly followed by the inferno of the Wars of the Roses. Even the rapturous commemorators of the Armada, again, will hardly claim that its repulse stood for aught but the patriotism of oppugnancy. To modern politics, then, let us come.

V

The last notable epoch of patriotic combination in our history is that of the war with France, begun in 1793 and carried on with intermissions till the final fall of Napoleon in 1815. And that epoch is still so near us in the spirit as well as in time, its affairs were carried on so much in the idiom of our own age and by our own Parliamentary methods, that it may specially well serve us as a test case. About its political outcome there is no question : it reduced to a small scope the play of intellectual disunion, in getting rid, for the moment, of the spirit of innovation, of protest, of social and intellectual criticism. Such a man as Coleridge, who in the early years of the war was on the critical side, but whose weaknesses steered him at length to that of convention and orthodoxy, could give thanks that the war had this unifying effect on the nation. And, indeed, though Fox and the remnant of his adherents held steadily to their general principle of peace and freedom, to the extent even of absenting themselves from the foregone proceedings of the House for months, mere faction might be said to have disappeared from the debates, and 'all were for the State,' so to say. The one ideal was enmity to France, enmity to the Revolution, enmity to Napoleon; and whatever ways of thought were even distantly associated with the revolutionary spirit and its French antecedents were not merely discountenanced but defamed, and not merely defamed but forcibly interfered with, and wherever possible savagely punished; that is to say, the heightening of patriotism meant a heightening of domestic malice where any ground of strife survived.

This very suppression of the small minority, to begin with, is visibly a long stride in that backward movement which we shall see to be a normal result of prolonged war in a nation previously progressive. There is but one way, be it repeated, in which a whole community can be raised and bettered from within, and that way begins in the free play of criticism, of new thought as against the old. Right or

Patriotism and Militarism

wrong, it must have a hearing; the alternative is not stand-still, but backing. And the sum of the rule of gag in the patriotic England of the Napoleonic age, whether we look at politics or at literature, is just a lapse from a state of comparative advance and activity to one of paralysis and retrogression. It is needless to frame anew the indictment item by item, to recite the tyrannies, the violences, the spoken and acted brutalities, or to recall the kind of language that stood for the voice of wisdom and authority in the closing years of Pitt and in the epoch of Lord Liverpool. To read the words spoken a hundred years ago by judges engaged in trying men for the offence of advocating political reforms is to hesitate over the premiss that that age, after all, spoke our idiom and worked our institutions. We seem for the moment to be re-reading the sayings of Hate-Good in the *Pilgrim's Progress*. To let one instance stand for a hundred, let the modern reader note the handling given in Scotland in 1794 to William Skirving, 'Secretary to the British Convention' of reformers. Skirving's spirit and aims are set forth in his declaration before the Lord Provost and Town Council of Edinburgh:

'My lord, a long time ago I perceived that the public mind in this country, as everywhere else, was in a remarkable state of irritation. I sought to divert this irritation into some channel which might moderate and regulate it. I urged, to the utmost of my influence, the association of the people, anxious to subject the public irritation to the control of delegates chosen by the people themselves, because of their greater wisdom and prudence.'

This was the literal truth : the agitation was absolutely orderly ; the sole reforms petitioned for were universal suffrage and annual Parliaments ; and the case for the prosecution consisted in a shameless pretence that words of warning to opponents as to the perils of the war policy were threats of massacre ; that an appeal for 'the peaceful restitution of their rights' to the people was seditious, in that it asserted they had been deprived of their natural rights ; that there was 'nothing more seditious' than the adoption of the title 'British Convention of the People'; and that 'the purpose of obtaining universal suffrage' was, in other words, 'the purpose of subverting the Government of Great Britain.' Such were the pleas of the Crown. The speech of the Lord Advocate on the evidence is a mere string of incoherent innuendos, of which the most precise is the assertion that universal suffrage would lead to a repetition of the French Revolution ; and the comments of the judges, one and all, con-

Patriotism and Militarism

sisted in the most grossly malignant aggravations of the charge, after the jury had given their verdict of Guilty. The speech of Lord Dunsinnan is typical of all, and thus it ran :

'My lords, this pannel has been found guilty, by a verdict of his country, of a crime of a very different nature, and of a more dangerous tendency than those common crimes which occur, and which are the daily subjects of trials in this court. My lords, it is the crime of sedition. It has been proved that these persons met for the purpose of subverting and altering the constitution of this country, under the pretence indeed of reform, but I say, really to subvert the constitution of the country ; and, my lords, from some other circumstances which came out yesterday, in the evening, and upon which the jury found him guilty' [evidence that Skirving's society had proposed to appoint an emergency committee, to act in private, and that there had been some talk of a possible French invasion], 'I confess I shudder to think of the horror that in certain events might have arisen from the train which this man and his accomplices had laid in different parts of this country. Thank God they are disappointed! Thank God we are still in possession of the laws to protect the constitution, and to establish the security of the subjects of it !'

The pretence of intended treason was obviously a stratagem, since, if that could be proved, the talk of subverting the constitution was beside the case. The real gravamen was simply the democratic attitude, and for that Skirving was sentenced to fourteen years' transportation. To this complexion had law and justice been brought under the British Constitution a hundred years ago, by the play of that sentiment of national union for which Coleridge later thanked God.

VI

It may be pleaded that these old judicial ferocities, infamous as they are, belonged to a period of intense strain and exasperation, in which the ruling class were in constant fear of such developments as they had seen in France; and that while their patriotism made them thus savage towards those whom they regarded as dangerous agitators, it did not stand for any lack of due sympathy with their fellow-citizens. Many people are thus ready to make excuses for cold British savagery on the part of the vowed guardians of pure justice, when they can see naught but ground for perpetual vituperation in the savageries to which the French Revolution was driven by the very menaces

Patriotism and Militarism

and conspiracies of its enemies. But let the excuses pass, and let us come to a crucial test. After the defeat of Napoleon in 1815, all reasonable fear of the revolutionary spirit as such was at an end, in England above all countries. Yet when, on the stoppage of the war expenditure and of the special demand for English products set up by the long disturbance of all industry on the Continent, a great distress fell upon industrial and agricultural England, it only needed the appearance of the suffering mass in the guise of famishing malcontents to arouse in the middle and upper class even such a hatred for their own poor as they had felt for the revolutionists of France. Sympathy was their weakest sentiment, and those who felt it were as nothing in weight and numbers to the malignant well-to-do majority. Twenty years of nominal national union in enmity to another nation had left the wealthy not more but less capable of beneficent fellow-feeling for their own 'kind' who had fought the fight with them. The English aristocrat had no more learned to care for his luckless countrymen than had Coriolanus in republican Rome. The old psychological process had had the old result. A generation of indulgence for the principle of enmity, with the usual growth of militant fraternity *ad hoc*, had left society much less fraternal as regarded the works of peace and mercy and building-up than it had been a generation before.

The 'Peterloo' massacre at Manchester, in 1819, served to exhibit the measure of fraternity existing in the nation that had defeated Napoleon. When a vast meeting of unarmed and orderly people had been brutally charged by cavalry, who sabred not only men, but women and children, Government and the Prince Regent applauded the act; and Lord Redesdale affirmed in a public letter that 'every meeting for radical reform was not merely a seditious attempt to undermine the existing constitution of government by bringing it into hatred and contempt, but was an overt act of treasonable conspiracy against that constitution of government, including the King as its head.' If anyone holds that our upper classes have outgrown that temper, let him but recall the episode of 'Black Sunday' in 1887, when heads were broken and life taken as wantonly, if not as wildly, as in 1819; and when gangs of middle-class men formed themselves into sets of special constables, lusting for more head-breaking, as zealously as any group of aristocrats ever swore the oath against the demos in ancient Athens. It was all sequent: in every case alike, hate does but breed hate; and an education in hating

Patriotism and Militarism

a national enemy proves to be but a training for callous or furious hostility at home.

Perhaps the most dramatic expression of the process within the century is that supplied by the Highland clearances which took place in the years 1815-20. The Highlands had supplied in singular abundance, relatively to their population, excellent troops for foreign service throughout the war. When the war was over, the disbanded soldiers could less than ever pay high rents for their poor crofts on hill and glen to their old landlords; and these patriots of the civilized sort had learned to regard high rents as the chief end of landlordism. So, without a word of sympathy from the aristocracy, whose battle the helot clansmen had fought, without a protective motion on the part of the Legislature, the lingering tribes were rooted out of their fatherland and shipped like cattle to Canada, or wheresoever else they could be cast, to shift for themselves. They had had their reward for patriotism, their part in the drama of pseudo-fraternity played once again by the primordial spirit of hate. It is only too true that their children remain 'loyal' and 'patriotic,' in the old sense, in their new homes. Such and so irrational are 'loyalty' and 'patriotism'; let the amateur of both make the most of it.

VII

It may help us further to a just notion of the matter if we turn for a moment from our own affairs to those of a country in which normal patriotism has latterly played a great part, under the guidance of a powerful statesman who has lately passed away. Before the advent of Bismarck the North-German States were, from the imperialist point of view, pitiable because 'disunited,' the assumption being that States speaking the same language ought to be united, not for any practical peaceful good that union brings, but for the sake of the consciousness of military power. Some Germans there were, certainly, who rationally desired federal union for the sake of the safeguard federation gives against mutual strife, as well as for security against invasion; but how little that view of the case counted for in the course of affairs was soon clear. If union was in that sense good for the North-German States, it was still better as between them and Austria, which also is in such large part German-speaking. But the Bismarckian ideal of union leant no more towards peace and goodwill than towards democracy and constitutionalism. The new union-maker knew all too well that the normal

Patriotism and Militarism 23

instinctive man cares for union first and last as a means to the gratification of the spirit of conflict; that he is a friend because he is an enemy; that he can best love in order to hate; and that what he craves as regards foreign States is not the sense of security but the pride of pre-eminent power. So the new apostle of brute force deliberately waged war in order to build up the kind of patriotism he wanted, and to swamp the party of reason and criticism which hampered him. First he wantonly attacked his weakest neighbour; and when he triumphed, the worse sort of his countrymen became in increasing numbers his partisans. That was the beginning of the new German union and the new German patriotism. The next step was to provoke to war another and stronger neighbour, but one known to be ill-prepared; and out of the new bloodshed there grew much more patriotism, and more of the spirit of union—the whole movement being deliberately directed to the aggrandisement of Bismarck's own State and King. For even North-German unity in the abstract he cared nothing; he had avowed that he would never consent to submerging the identity of Prussia in a coalition: the only permissible unity for him should be a unity of which Prussia was the head, with her King glorified as Kaiser. The man's every ideal was on the plane of the Middle Ages; and he succeeded because most men are still morally and psychologically on the plane of the Middle Ages, with but a veneer of modern science to disguise them to themselves. After creating two needless wars, he set himself to induce a third —the bloodiest and worst of all, again with a neighbour whom he knew to be ill-prepared. For his own part, being the one European statesman who was all along deliberately scheming evil, he was prepared for the utmost effort and for every contingency. And now came his crowning triumph. As one war had enabled him to bring to a confederation under Prussia the group of North-German States, who otherwise would not have consented, so the ecstasy of the pan-German triumph over France carried the Allied States to the pitch of hailing the Prussian King German Emperor. It was never honest mutual goodwill that wrought such a consummation: it was the primeval lust of enmity and the flushed passion of victory that brought about the symbolic unification : the Germans had fraternized in order to crush the French, and they sealed the fraternization with crown and empire in the pride of the achievement.

And this is really the supreme illustration of

Patriotism and Militarism

the play of 'patriotism' for the modern world. Led thus brutally to wade through blood to military and political union, the German nation is regarded not only by its own majority, but by the majority elsewhere, as having attained the highest felicity in any nation's reach. That a nation should make itself drunk with the pride of power as a man makes himself drunk with brandy — this is acclaimed without misgiving as a glorious experience, fit to arouse that 'envy of surrounding nations' which in previous platitude was the appanage of the British Constitution. The mere proof of the possession of superior power, a certificate which, as regards individuals, passes among civilized men as the ambition and the mark of the pugilist, or, at best, of the mere duellist or the mere athlete—this attestation, made applicable to one nation as against another, is held to have in it something ethically ennobling; and the banal pride in it, dubbed 'patriotism,' passes for an incontestable virtue. Here is our ethical problem.

We shall have to consider later the results of this embodiment of the idea and the sanction of patriotism in the act of war and the institution of armaments. Meanwhile, we are tracing it to its psychological roots and connotations. And we are already fully entitled to say that the whole processus is animalistic, and the whole associations vulgar. In the supreme case of Germany the vulgarity is fitly flagrant. The Man of Blood and Iron, the Strong Man of the Carlylean gospel, the brutal wielder of brute force, was always a magnified flunkey, changing his livery thrice a day, playing the obedient giant to the King who signed the letters and made the moves the giant dictated. It is as 'true German servant of Wilhelm I.' that in the end the giant ethically esteems himself: not as the servant of Germany or the German people; still less of humanity; least of all as the self-realizing free spirit of German philosophy. Where the giant prostrated himself, *a fortiori* Germany did; and this generation has seen growing up in due progression what a recalcitrant German spirit has described as the cult of God the Father, God the Son, and God the Grandson, which three in the Grandson are one. It is perhaps not more vulgar than the phenomena of royalism in England: that, indeed, could hardly be; but it is more gross, more primitive—as much more aggressively offensive as German militarism is more powerful than English. And patriotism gilds it all. The personal tyranny of the reigning Kaiser, a tyranny meaner than the first Napoleon's, and much more inquisitorial than that of the third, stands for the moral whole created and symbolized by Sedan; and a great people mutely winces under a young despot's whip in the name of the blood-bought 'unity' in which 'patriotism' still sees the crowning good. Not for ever, surely—perhaps not for long; since already the extremity of the evil strengthens that systematic antagonism which, in the name of Socialism, most profoundly countervails mere patriotism and all its works. That resistance, evoking as it does in turn a bitterness of social ill-will against itself not easily to be matched elsewhere, is the last testimony to the futility of the patriotism of enmity as a solvent of domestic division, and as a builder-up of even civic fraternity. But it is for the next century to reveal whether the ancient insanity is not again to triumph, as it did under the regimen of Bismarck, over the higher aspirations of enlightened men in the most laboriously thoughtful of modern nations. Led by Bismarck, Germany's work has been to turn back all social and political progress, and to set up a systematic reign of militarism, which means force as nearly mindless as is compatible with successful direction, in place of what had seemed a growing disregard for the lower instincts, and a confused but gradually clarifying ideal of international peace. The nation nominally the most philosophic has been made to exemplify the most unphilosophic of all political ideals. If the same nation should in turn accomplish the most thorough undoing of the reign of force and enmity, it will have ground for a satisfaction as much nobler than the old as the new results will be more blessed. But in the meantime, with Bismarck dead, Bismarckism still darkens our every vista ; and States that had once seemed most alien to his ideals seem grown capable of pursuing, if not of realizing them.

VIII

Leaving, however, for later contemplation that aspect of the matter, let us take one more view of the nature of patriotism as seen operating in our own politics. Those who habitually make the assumption of the nobility and beneficence of the instinct in its natural and spontaneous form, as the assertion of the Will-to-Live of a given community or race, might be expected to acclaim it wherever it appears —in the affairs of other groups as well as in their own. And the patriotism-mongers of England do, as we have seen, applaud it in Germany ; nay, they mostly applauded it in Italy when Italians were struggling against

Patriotism and Militarism

the Austro-Germans. Italy and Germany are far off; besides, the Italians fought Austria, which never had much attraction for England, and the Germans fought the French, towards whom many Englishmen still feel little goodwill—having, it must be owned, no great encouragement thereto from the normal attitude of the French journals. It is when we turn to the case of Ireland that the ethical quality of the patriotic instinct reveals itself. If English patriots, so called, had in them any pure sympathy for struggling patriotism as such, any genuine moral inspiration for their own instinct, they would recognise in Irish nationalist aspirations the very virtue they profess to revere. These are the very circumstances in which, from any point of view, patriotism must in justice be reckoned sanative. To the eye of the political rationalist, it is in such a case a force whereby a people is combined for its betterment, stimulated to a higher level of moral self-consciousness, fired to a joint effort which means no menace towards any other people, but seeks sheer benefit without any offset of destruction. Here, if ever, should it have the endorsement of good men. To the average patriot, again, the desire of a people with common traditions and common needs to secure as full a measure of self-rule as is possessed by those with whom they are in nominal union—this should surely figure as patriotism in its most attractive form, unless it be that his sympathies are only to be aroused by blood-letting or the effort thereto; by the plots of Poles and the insurrections of Italians. But we know very well that the average English patriot had no more consideration for armed Fenianism than he has for unarmed Nationalism. The utter egoism, the unintelligent animalism of his instinct comes out the moment another man's instinct clashes with it. Patriotism for him means hatred of other men's patriotism the moment they thereby incommode him, albeit they only ask him to give them in reality the rights he accords them in name. Bitterly, nay, furiously, he vilifies in them the passion he applauds in himself; professing at times, perhaps, for once in a way to apply to the whole question the test of utility, but offering in its name only pleas which are the expression of his own naïve and lawless egoism.

Scratch thus the patriot, and you find the pirate; test the devotee of freedom, and you find the insolent oppressor. And to no one who has much meditated on the normal moralities of men is the upshot disconcerting. What other outcome should there be from

Patriotism and Militarism 31

the self-glorifying parade of a primeval instinct, taken without purification by man from beast? If the braggart among men be an offence to the civilized moral sense, how shall nations satisfy the first principles of civilized ethics when they set to themselves the pose and the phrase of the braggart as a discipline and an ideal? Not from the thistles of the savage prime shall be gathered the fruits of international civility. If men, as constituents of nations, will not consent to think and reason for the whole as they do for themselves and each other singly, they must fatally, as nations, remain at the moral level of the human animal, scientific only for the work of mischief, licensing itself to be brutal and irrational in mass while claiming to denounce brutality and eliminate unreason in the individual. And the individual will all the while assuredly reflect the ideals of the mass.

IX

In a recent work of realistic fiction, a study of life in the criminal class in the East End of London, there is presented, probably without the author's knowledge, and doubtless without his intention, a singularly clear vision of the nature and operation of the passion of patriotism.

The book in question is Mr. Arthur Morrison's masterly story, *A Child of the Jago*, one of those fictions which, exhibiting to most of us a phase of life of which we have known nothing, almost irresistibly convince us of their trustworthiness. Obviously, such an impression ought on second thoughts to be revised; and one sees cause to suspect that Mr. Morrison's picture of life in 'the Jago' makes out that sort of existence to be more symmetrical, more sequent, more homogeneous in its kind, than it really is, even as the novel of normal life unduly simplifies that. But this criticism, supposing it to be valid as against the structure of Mr. Morrison's story, which is skilfully composed in the contemporary impressionist manner, does not, I think, affect that aspect of it to which I am here calling notice. Here the study is either wholly false or substantially true.

'The Jago,' it should be explained for any reader of these pages who may not know the book, is a certain group of old streets (now demolished) in the Bethnal Green district, inhabited mostly by habitual criminals. As against the law-abiding and law-enforcing world, this population is spontaneously united, fraternal, and co-operative. The police are the common enemy, to be lied to, baffled, and if

Patriotism and Militarism 33

possible 'bashed,' when they cross the Jago frontier. But this is what might have been expected. What comes upon us as a revelation, and yet as a luminously intelligible expression of natural law, is the fact that the people of the Jago live in chronic feud with those of a neighbouring group of streets, generalized as 'Dove Lane,' whereof the inhabitants differ only partially from them in respect of not being all thieves, or not always thieving. In this feud every 'Jago' is ready at a moment's notice to fight in rank with his neighbours against any body of Dove-Laners. After a pitched battle has raged itself out, a process sometimes taking several days, the feud for a time slumbers, and may even be patched up by a semi-formal treaty between the leading spirits of both sides, who duly fraternize in a representative public-house of either territory. Peace will then last for an indefinite time, till it shall be broken by a drunken brawl between individuals of the two groups, or as a result of a diffused feeling that it has lasted long enough, and that the other side need beating.

But while the slum is thus united against the 'natural enemy,' and the war-cry, 'Hold tight, Jago,' will rally all the blackguards of the place for the geographical conflict, 'the Jago' has a feud within itself, as furious and as frequent

34   Patriotism and Empire

as that between Jago and Dove-Laner. Two of the leading scoundrels of the Jago are Billy Rann and Billy Leary, and all Jagory chronically divides into Rann and Leary factions, which 'bash' each other for days at a time as zealously as if one of the sides were of Dove Lane, the women going into the fray, and even outdoing the males of their species in ferocity of method. When a Rann-Leary battle has raged itself out, or is curtailed by an act of manslaughter that elicits the police, the factions relapse into fraternity for awhile, and are ready at due notice to make common cause against the Dove-Laners.

And there is yet one more complication. Now and then, when the thieving business is depressed, the bulk of the manifold rascality loafing about Jagodom will suddenly decide on a filibustering raid through the main streets, in the course of which every isolated inhabitant found in the open is hustled, robbed, and if need be 'bashed,' the proceeds of this 'crowded hour of glorious life' being divided as honourably as may be, among the raiders. Jagoism thus presents, in its one-horse hell, all the variations undergone in normal society by the animal instinct which figures now as egoism, now as partisanism, now as patriotism. In the Jago, as in the larger world, each is for himself,

Patriotism and Militarism 35

and the devil is specially welcome to the hindmost. But the Jago, like the average citizen, is a social animal, prone to combination—for a purpose ; so he is ready for an occasional syndicate of thievery, good for a whole forenoon, during which he will rob indifferently Jago and Gentile. Again, he has his hereditary family or feudal bias, and when a Rann-Leary row is ' on ' he takes his part with all the alacrity of a knight distinguishing between Guelph and Ghibeline, or White Rose and Red. Finally, though at a pinch he may ' bash ' his neighbour or rob his neighbour's wife or child, he is a true, loyal, patriotic Jago as against all Dove-Laners.

The question arises, In what respect is the patriotism of the Jago less rational or less respectable than the patriotism of the Jingo? And the answer must be that the only difference is one of social status and prestige. Psychologically the two forms of feeling are identical. Passing for moral inspirations of the most unquestionable kind, they are equally animal with the sympathies and animosities of cats and dogs, and they are alike belied by the daily life of those who exhibit them. When bitter enemies join hands on the strength of a common hatred for an enemy outside, they are more or less confident that they are doing a fine thing. They might as well glorify themselves over the animosities which divide them when the 'natural' enemy is out of sight; and, indeed, they do so, though they reserve the approving title of patriotism for the animosity that is cherished in common. Once more, it is not brotherhood, or sympathy, or goodwill that unites the general population in a flush of passion against another population: the ostensible brotherhood of the moment is merely a passing product of the union of egoisms. The men who prate most of patriotism and 'the Empire,' and who dwell most habitually on our 'natural' hostility to Russia, or to Germany, or to France, are as a rule conspicuous for their indifference to the well-being of the mass of their fellow-countrymen, and for the virulence of their ill-feeling towards those of another way of thinking in politics. Animosity of one sort or the other is the spring of all their politics. In a general way, indeed, they desire good trade for the country at large, and they rejoice when 'our' trade is in better case than that of other countries; but they would not move a finger so to alter the social structure that the working mass should gain in wealth and comfort; rather they resent the workers' claim as they resent foreign competition in land-grabbing. At most they may help in times of special distress as do

Patriotism and Militarism

the Jagos, who get up a 'break' to finance a brother thief newly out of gaol, and not yet earning an income. But as regards anything like all-round sympathy, they are positively inferior to the Jagos, who are pretty much of one class, and whose domestic feuds are intermittent, not steadfastly active jealousies.

It would seem, then, that the 'good' society has little cause to plume itself on its superiority to the 'bad,' as regards the moral springs of its international action. The inspiration of the patriotic Jingo, however different in literary colour, is just the inspiration of the blackguard Jago—as far away from reason, from self-criticism, from the spirit of righteousness. The maxim, 'our country, right or wrong,' is but the wording of a sentiment which the Jago acts upon without thinking that any formula is necessary. And it would seem to be a safe inference that while our polity turns largely on ideals or principles which we hold in common with burglars and bullies, our society will continue to exhibit plain phases of the predatory and brutish stages of civilization.

X

It may be well, before leaving this side of the matter, to take account of the possible protest that civilized patriotism has in it elements of purely benevolent feeling, and that if not strictly altruistic—some may perhaps insist that it *is* properly altruistic—it is so far a mental state of goodwill and aspiration, of pleasure in good, and of natural admiration and social sympathy, that it cannot reasonably be likened even remotely to the instincts of thieves and ruffians. Let it be observed on this that the word 'patriotism' means nothing if not a specialization of our sympathies, a caring much more for our own people than for any other. It does not stand for the mere necessary restriction of most of the display of our goodwill to those who are nearest us. We call philanthropist the man who, while practically most concerned with his own people, yet gives out a doctrine or a precept framed in the interest of all mankind; the name of patriot is normally and naturally given to the man who either fights his own country's battle or specially strives to put his country at an advantage as against others. To say of the philanthropist, as we may well do, that he is the true patriot, is really to urge a moral criticism on the lines of the present argument; it is not an agreement to make the word 'patriotism' mean something else than it normally has done. As long as the thing, the

Patriotism and Militarism

proclivity, subsists throughout the world, it must have a name, and we are here employing that name at its ordinary value.

If, then, it be claimed for patriotism that it involves certain quite laudable frames of mind, the answer is that, to be patriotic at all, a mood of benevolence must be distinctly restrictive and exclusive—that is, must connote a conscious withholding of some goodwill from other communities. But I can conceive its being argued that a decent and cultured patriotism is rather a giving out of special goodwill on the stimulus of fellow-citizenship than a lessening of what would otherwise be given to the foreigner; that it is not a subtraction from, but an addition to, the total amount of human sympathy of which the average man is capable.

Let this claim, then, be tested over a really good example of cultured patriotism, which has already come under general notice at the hands of a champion of culture. It was in his latter years that Mr. Matthew Arnold, discussing the career and work of Tolstoy, thus delivered himself on the subject of the sensitiveness and self-consciousness of Americans :

'But the Americans, as we know, are apt to set them at rest in the manner of my friend Colonel Higginson of Boston. "As I take it, Nature said some years since : 'Thus far the English is my best race, but we have had

Englishmen enough; we need something with a little more buoyancy than the Englishman; let us lighten the structure, even at some peril in the process. Put in one drop more of nervous fluid, and make the American.' With that drop a new range of promise opened on the human race, and a lighter, finer, more highly organized type of mankind was born." People who by this sort of thing give rest to their sensitive and busy self-consciousness may very well, perhaps, be on their way to great material prosperity, to great political power; but they are scarcely on the right way to a great literature, a serious art.'

This not unskilful attack might be met by, let me also say, my friend Colonel Higginson with a sufficiently effective *tu quoque*, in respect of certain of Mr. Arnold's own indulgences in patriotic elation. For it was Mr. Arnold who, after many sound counsels to his countrymen to take note of their shortcomings as beside other Europeans, thus glorified the Church of England in an essay on that institution:

'Show me any other great Church of which a chief actor and luminary has a sentence like this sentence, *splendide verax*, of Butler's: "Things are what they are, and the consequences of them will be what they will be; why, then, should we wish to be deceived?" . . . Intensely Butlerian as this sentence is, yet Butler came to it because he is English, because at the bottom of his nature lay such a fund of integrity.'

There is, of course, nothing out of the way in this exhibition. Just as French writers, Hugo among them, tell us complacently that it

Patriotism and Militarism

is the special characteristic of Paris to be 'steeped in good sense,' so do our English writers chronically illustrate our good sense by proclaiming it. Macaulay reminds us of 'that masculine and full-grown robustness of mind, that equally diffused intellectual health which, if our national partiality does not mislead us, has peculiarly characterized the great men of England;' and Mr. Leslie Stephen courageously assures us that Swift and Dr. Johnson 'are alike in that shrewd, humorous common-sense which seems to be the special endowment of the English race'—a precious proposition, fitly proved. Arnold is but falling into line with the immemorial national procession, wearing the customary beatific smile with the customary ineptitude. And if this sort of thing be permissible to an English critic without demur from common-sense, Colonel Higginson must be well within his rights in claiming for Americans such a trifle as an extra drop of vivacity. But when he reflects how much more apt is such a claim on his side to be overcrowed on the other by countervailing claims than to be conceded in a spirit of teachable modesty, he will perhaps grant me that even if it were as true for the States in general as it probably is for cultured Boston, it was after all not quite worth pressing. No doubt he has the justification, urged by him in his searching and intimately suggestive volume of papers on *The New World and the New Book*, that some Americans may still be the better of a little encouragement to their self-respect under the pressure of English assumptions—an excuse which was entirely lacking to Mr. Arnold, on his own reiterated testimony. Colonel Higginson's claim, too, is bottomed on a great deal of Mr. Arnold's own criticism of Anglo-Saxon density, as set forth, in particular, in the essay *On the Study of Celtic Literature*.

But is not all this just a clinching proof of the perverting influence of the patriotic sentiment? That sentiment it was which, reviving in the elderly English critic, made him at one moment false to his own principles and his earlier enlightened practice, to the point of an absolutely absurd display of national vanity, and at another moment made him unreflectively resent a much more reasonable flight of nationalist self-satisfaction on the part of a friendly American.

No good is done to anybody in England or anywhere else, and certainly no healthy discipline is given to the boaster's own intelligence, by such a boast as that about the peculiarly Anglican character of the disposition to avoid self-deception. But if that be granted of Arnold's claim for Englishmen, it would seem to follow that Colonel Higginson's claim for Americans, however just, is not the most educative of his judgments. If in itself it could serve to hearten diffident Americans, the service would be only the more likely to be undone by Arnold's counter-sarcasm, which in the terms of the case would be doubly disheartening to such temperaments. Americans in general, however, really do not need to be encouraged to think well of themselves any more than do Englishmen; rather they have, in the mass, like their kinsmen, self-satisfaction to spare. To flatter them, then, is surely no part of a wise American's business, not to say of his duty. The more one meditates the matter, the more one is moved to prescribe for one's nation, as for one's self, the exercise of self-criticism in preference to the exercise of self-praise. If Shakespeare could see fit to brood on his own deficiencies,

'Desiring this man's art and that man's scope,'

the nations which read and acclaim him may well take the same medicine for their collective flatulences. For nervous depression there is always handy the safe tonic of simple criticism of the faults of other nations.

44 Patriotism and Empire

There was a time, no doubt, when educated Americans, as distinguished from ordinary patriots, needed encouragement from their men of culture to stand upon their intellectual birthright. Poe, Emerson, and Whitman, from their different standpoints saw the need and ministered to it—Poe pointing to the intellectual weakness of the current English criticism, before which Americans bowed; Emerson distilling what was intellectually valid in the patriotic sense of the Republic's importance; Whitman poetically transmuting patriotism into something nobler and rarer. But observe, first, the virtue, in all three of these writers, of the saving grace of their intellectual motive, and next the peril, in different cases, of the normal patriotic motive working in the same direction. Poe, though a little touched with local or Southern prejudice, was incapable of mere sentimental patriotism, and did but urge independence on his countrymen in regard to English criticism, as he would have urged it on any school of them as against the Transcendentalists. Emerson was much less of an emotionalist, much less of a vessel of instinct, in his politics than in his philosophy; in reality he philosophized politics for his fellow-republicans. Whitman, in some aspects somewhat of an 'American Americanizing,'

Patriotism and Militarism 45

really struck a note which, intellectually, far outsoars that of mere patriotism, and has thus had scant welcome from American patriots.

Very different in temperamental basis from all of these utterances was Mr. Lowell's essay *On a Certain Condescension in Foreigners*, where the chief inspiration was obviously the predisposition to condescend in turn. Here we have patriotic self-love retaliating on foreign self-esteem, instinct clashing with instinct, with the result of yielding much heat and little light, though Lowell was much more of a wit and of a humorist than any of the others. Dialectically the essay is a marvel of incoherence. Again and again it shows a full cognizance of the fact that the foreign impertinences complained of had always been well matched by American impertinences; that democratic arrogance had always held its own against aristocratic, boast for boast and insult for insult; yet the middle-aged man of letters must needs fume, nay, foam, on behalf of the geographical 'we,' even in the act of avowing his incommunity with myriads of his neighbours. In this allocution he treats with downright anger propositions in regard to American life, such as he has himself made in another essay; and much of his argument is a rebuttal of his own previous utterance.* The outcome is a see-saw of splenetic admission and more splenetic aspersion, logically amounting only to the proposition 'You're another,' and furnishing to the reflective reader no moral profit whatsoever, save, it may be, that of having seen how such matters ought not to be handled. Even the quality of the writing, excellent as Lowell's always is—excellent in spite of an occasional flaw; excellent even in the too frequent claptrap—does not make amends for the bad thinking. The soreness to which it so confusedly testifies is the measure of the vanity of the primary passion of patriotism at best, and of its fatal potency, when sentimentally cherished, to evict humour from the head no less than good-humour from the heart. His resentment of jocular foreign condescension never taught Lowell to bate his jocular condescension towards foreigners — never, at least, in his writings, where Celt and Teuton, French and German, Scotch and English, are in turn joked about with a robust complacency. Yet, how grievously are his withers wrung by the chance poke of the English pilgrim's staff!

* Compare the opening pages of the essay, *A Great Public Character* with that above discussed, which immediately precedes it in *My Study Windows*. But the *Condescension* essay itself betrays the spirit divided against itself.

Patriotism and Militarism 47

There is yet another way of 'encouraging' the diffident American spirit, a way which has one obvious advantage over Mr. Lowell's, but which in turn is open to damaging criticism—I mean the attitude taken by Washington Irving in a letter to Motley, as late as 1857. There must have been already a good deal of plucking-up of heart in the States before the cosmopolitan Irving could be moved to write thus :

> 'You are properly sensible of the high calling of the American press, that rising tribunal before which the history of all nations is to be revised and rewritten, and the judgment of past ages to be corrected or confirmed.'

The first and perhaps the worst trouble about deliverances of this kind is that they are extremely apt to elicit European ridicule of the kind that Dickens poured out on American self-praise in *Martin Chuzzlewit*, a book which to this day counts for harm in English popular culture. I will not, however, dwell on that kind of rejoinder, much less echo it; rather let us seek for a judicial verdict from our common-sense. Irving, one presumes, did not by 'press' mean merely 'newspaper press': he must have meant serious literature in general; so I will not raise the question whether American journalism any more than European has realized what used to be expected of it. If, however, the proposition be taken in its most plausible sense, will it bear criticism? Irving's idea was that the democratic spirit could and would fitly sit in judgment on feudal and monarchic history, institutions, ethics, ideals. So be it; but what is to give the American press a monopoly of that spirit, that tribunal? Mere political democracy, as thus far evolved in the States, is a very imperfect rectification of social inequality; and a far profounder criticism of the evils of the European past and present has been latterly produced in Europe itself than that hitherto current in the States. Marx and Morris, surely, cut deeper than either Irving or Motley dreamt of going; and their criticism has thus far found much more acceptance in old-world Germany and England than in the States. The late Mr. Bellamy brilliantly took up their parable; but he seems to have had more sympathizers, proportionally, in England than in his own country.

All this, be it understood, is no impeachment of the civilization of the United States. The relative tardiness of Socialistic thought there is simply the expression of the greater elasticity there of the economic conditions for individualism than in Europe. But it all goes to suggest that the civilization of the future is hardly likely to be a triumphal march of the unchanged Republic, under President, Senate,

Patriotism and Militarism 49

and Congress, far in advance of a forever unchanged Europe, mostly monarchic and aristocratic to the end. My honoured friend Dr. Moncure Conway, nearly a generation ago, urged upon his fellow-countrymen of the States that their constitution exemplified certain 'Republican Superstitions.' As a convinced republican, I venture to say with him that in the mere matter of constitution-making there is much to be done before the States can satisfy the tests of scientific democracy. How far are we, then, from a state of things in which the mere quality of being American can give any criticism a precedence or prerogative in the intellectual world? When Irving wrote, the impeachment of slavery in Dickens's *American Notes* stood facile to the hand of any man who cared to make the retort; to-day, one fears, the Socialists of Europe, under whatever rule they live, will be hardly less ready than was Dickens to repugn the notion of an American Supreme Court in the world of ideas. Many of them, indeed, would repugn it unintelligently, undervaluing the factor they dismissed. The judgment passed on American life by Huysmans, that fine flower of old-world decadence, has really less rational weight than the claim of Irving. But there is only the more need that we should all alike get over the nationalistic attitude, and drop all judgments which attribute special powers and special impotences to given communities as such.

Why cannot instructed men everywhere agree to substitute for all other claims to jurisdiction the claim of universal Reason? Colonel Higginson argues, justly enough, that for some Americans 'cosmopolitanism' comes to signify just Europeanism; that they do not stand for a true cosmopolitanism even when asking for it. Be it so; is not the solution still a substitution of a universal test for an avowed particularism? Is there any rest for the spirit of wisdom in a nationalist self-exaltation? Why should any of us go on separately taking the old perverse pleasure in the notion that the mass of mankind will for ever be inferior in wit, wisdom, and well-being to our own particular nation? Is there really any sane comfort for an instructed American in believing that Europe will always be feudal, undemocratic, ethically backward, as compared with his own people? If his education be worthy of the name, he has learned much from living Europeans, and he is aware that many living Europeans are as well fitted to sit in judgment on American history as he can be to sit in judgment on theirs. He cannot well suppose that they are going meekly to bow, for themselves and for Europe, under the verdict of the amiable Irving. He will wish, indeed, to see developed in America as large a body of experts, of capable thinkers, as exists in Europe, as the intelligent men of every nation wish to see their own people make up leeway in the matters in which they are backward. But that very sense of intellectual parity with other communities which is, or would be, so comforting and sustaining to him, is it not equally so to the others? Why, then, should he wish to see them deprived of it in the future? The only intelligible reason why is just the old passion of patriotism, a passion in itself the potential solvent and negation of culture, in the sense that it turns to naught the best fruits thereof. In reality, the one kind of progress which in these days would represent a moral superiority on the part of any one civilized nation over any other would be precisely the subordination or subdual of the spirit of patriotism by political reason. And that step does not at the moment appear, in the terms of the case, to be nearer accomplishment in the New World than in the Old. Rather, the New World has to pass, however much more rapidly, through stages of error in which the Old has long dwelt. The problem, then, cannot be too searchingly discussed, in either hemisphere, by the lovers of light and of civilization.

XI

As it happens, the people of the United States are in a fair way to follow those of the United Kingdom into a snare that is laid for all peoples who can greatly enlarge their bounds or their numbers. They are like to suffer, as so many Englishmen have suffered, from the giddiness that goes with sheer political extension. In England the malady, which a generation ago had seemed in a way to be cured, grows more offensively prevalent every day, till the reaction seems overdue. And as this trouble is manifestly a malignant form of the old affection of patriotism, it calls for some special notice in these pages. To put the case shortly, if nationalism is bad, imperialism is worse. If to intoxicate one's self on fatherland be unwholesome, to grow drunken on empire is pestilent.

On the English side, the contagion is assiduously quickened by certain men of letters, who combine a special gift of speech with the ideals and the information of an average boy. Singly and collectively, they stand for the type of the Barbarian Sentimentalist. We may take as the most distinguished members of the school Mr. Kipling and Mr. Henley, the first

Patriotism and Militarism 53

a briliant story-teller, who passes for a poet with the unpoetical; the second an admirable artist in verse, who passes for a prophet with the unprophetical, and for a politician with the incapable of politics. It would be hard to find two men of literary genius with less of rational insight into the life-conditions of the political organism to which they belong. To their eyes, the stupendous problem of industrial continuance, which is the problem of life for millions of overdriven men, resolves itself into a kind of military pageant, with occasional fighting to lend it dignity; and for them, accordingly, all political philosophy begins and ends in the literary picturesque. This is how Mr. Henley prefaces a work on *Imperialism* by one of his school :

'We have renewed our old pride in the Flag, our old delight in the thought of a good thing done by a good man of his hands, our old faith in the ambitions and traditions of the race. I doubt, for instance, if outside politics (and, perhaps, the Stock Exchange), there be a single Englishman who does not rejoice in the triumph of Mr. Rhodes; even as I believe that there is none, inside or out of politics, who does not feel the prouder for his kinship with Sir Herbert Kitchener. And the reason is on the surface. To the national conscience, drugged so long and so long bewildered and bemused, such men as Rhodes and Kitchener are heroic Englishmen. The one has added some hundreds of thousands of square miles to the Empire, and is neck-deep in the work of consolidating that he has got, and of taking more. The other is wiping out the great dishonour that overtook us at Khartoum, at the same time that he is "reaching down from the north" to Buluwayo, and preparing the way of them that will change a place of skulls into a province of peace. Both are great, and that is much. But both are, after all, but types; and that is more. We know now, Mr. Kipling aiding, that all the world over are thousands of the like temper, the like capacity for government, the like impatience of anarchy; and that all the world over, these—each one according to his vision and his strength—are doing Imperial work at Imperial wages: the chance of a nameless death, the possibility of distinction, the certainty that the effect is worth achieving, and will surely be achieved.'

Observe that the peace-making imperial life here preached and panegyrized depends for its very existence on the continued supply of fighting barbarism. Without barbarian territory to steal and militant barbarians to shoot, the fabric of tinfoil glory passes away as a peepshow. Blessed are the powder-and-shot peacemakers, for they shall always go on inheriting more earth, is Mr. Henley's gospel. Our sentimentalist, himself a barbarian, proclaims a Jehad against barbarism; but without barbarism to fight he is at a dead stand. The glorious task of the Imperialist, as here set forth, consists in subduing the Soudan, and so on; but when there are no more Soudans to subdue, in the terms of the case, 'Imperial work' is at an end, and there is nothing left for

Patriotism and Militarism 55

the 'national conscience' but to become once more 'drugged, and bewildered, and bemused.' By a series of Soudans only can we be annually saved. So absolutely childish a gospel is hardly a subject for serious argument, but it is among the possibilities of our chaotic system that such mindless rhodomontade may, in a bad hour, turn the balance of political movement from sanity to delirium.

The outstanding result of the conflict of the hand-to-mouth Opportunisms into which both Liberalism and Toryism have resolved themselves in England since Gladstone and Disraeli took them in tutelage, is that none of our statesmen have any ostensible political philosophy at all, save in so far as a few on the Liberal side at times recall the lore of their early teachers. Men who were at least trained in the Liberal school are seen formulating theories of international action which might have been hatched by Disraeli in one of his earlier romances. In this state of things it needs only a sufficiently evil conjuncture of circumstances to enable a Moses of the Music-Hall, with perhaps a few Aarons of the Areopagus, to start a Jingo crusade in which the nation may march as straight to dire disaster as ever did any host of 'drugged, bemused, and bewildered' fanatics in the Dark Ages. Eloquent ignorance has wrought such things in the past, and may compass them again. To rule or conserve an empire in these days requires first and last sound economic science, and a calm grasp of the manifold lesson of political history. Our energumens of empire, all the while, know as much of economic science as did the Mahdi, and are about as fit as he to instruct a civilized people.

To what economic wisdom they can attain when they put their inspiration and their information together may be gathered from an indescribable article which appeared a year or two ago in a leading English journal. The writer undertook to set forth the contingent destinies of Great Britain and Germany in the matter of their commerce. Comparing the commercial rivalry of the two nations with an affectation of cynical impartiality, he pronounces:

'A million petty disputes build up the greatest cause of war the world has ever seen. If Germany were extinguished to-morrow, the day after to-morrow there is not an Englishman in the world who would not be the richer. Nations have fought for years over a city or a right of succession; must they not fight for two hundred and fifty million pounds of yearly commerce?'

This is the economic premiss, absolute absurdity affirmed with absolute confidence,

Patriotism and Militarism 57

the political economy of the Dark Ages enounced with the glibness of the *Pall Mall* paragraphist. He regards trade as a process of securing tribute, and holds that the extinction of one trading nation enriches the others to the extent of its whole turnover—as who should say that an individual tradesman best adds to his income by murdering his richest customers.

'Prince Bismarck has long recognised what at length the people of England are beginning to understand—that in Europe there are two great, irreconcilable, opposing forces, two great nations who would make the whole world their province, and who would levy from it the tribute of commerce.'

It may be that Prince Bismarck also cherished that hallucination of the mess-room. He, too, as we have said, held by the political philosophy of the Dark Ages; and we know with what fury his brother-in-arms, Moltke, saw the industrial prosperity of France and the coincident distress in Germany after the war milliards had been paid and pocketed. To these two paladins it doubtless looked like witchcraft. The worst of the matter is that minds capable of this solution of the problem of international trade are probably incapable of mastering any other. It is of no avail to point to such a one in England that with England Germany does much more trade than with any other nation; that Germany is the third-best of England's customers, apart from India and Australia; that Anglo-German trade has increased by millions in ten years; that the English imports from Germany exceed the exports by several millions, showing that Germany, like France and the United States, pays England 'tribute' on English investments in Germany, whereas the figures show that British capital is annually being deported to South Africa in excess of the returns; that Germany is a bigger customer for Britain than South Africa and Canada together, and not far below Australia; and, finally, that Germany is far less capacitated to intercept English trade than are the United States, which far exceed England in stores of coal and iron, whereas Germany is in these our inferior, though, on the other hand, the States pay an enormous annual 'tribute' on English investments. Our medieval patriot, indeed, will not, even if he assimilates the facts as to the United States, propose that we should undertake to destroy them in order to increase our incomes. His medieval economics all the while are but a gloss on his militarist instinct and his patriotism, which together breed in him the desire to fight Germany, because Germany irritates him, and he thinks England can defeat her at sea. He can vaguely realize that American naval power is indefinitely expansible; so the American interception of British commerce must perforce be permitted. But he believes he or 'we' can safely insult the Germans, and he thus proceeds to do so:

'What Bismarck realized, and what we too may soon come to see, is that not only is there the most real conflict of interests between England and Germany, but that England is the only Great Power who could fight Germany without tremendous risk and without doubt of the issue. Her partners in the Triple Alliance would be useless against England: Austria, because she could do nothing; Italy, because she dare not lay herself open to attack by France. The growth of Germany's fleet has done no more than to make the blow of England fall on her more heavily. The ships would soon be at the bottom of the sea or in convoy to English ports; Hamburg and Bremen, the Kiel Canal and the Baltic ports, would lie under the guns of England, waiting until the indemnity were settled. Our work over, we need not even be at the pains to alter Bismarck's words to Ferry, and to say to France and Russia, "Seek some compensation. Take inside Germany whatever you like: you can have it."'

And the article ends with 'Germaniam esse delendam.' Thus are peace on earth, goodwill among men, commerce, and the science of commerce, promoted among us by the imperial and patriotic press. We can hear Mr. Henley rejoicing at the promulgation of such a healing and luminous gospel to his hitherto drugged, bemused, and bewildered countrymen; and we can imagine Mr. Kipling turning it into his psalmodic verse, with its rhythms of the drum and its modulations of the trumpet.

The people of the United States, clearly, cannot be worse bemused by their megalomaniacs than are their kin beyond seas; but the malady being 'most incident' to human nature, they were bound to catch it. A certain sort of megalomania belonged to the early stage of Western expansion, the expansive citizen being apt to feel that the greatness of the continent in some way reflected greatness on him. 'Even during our war,' wrote Lowell in one of his dispassionate hours, 'in the midst of that almost unrivalled stress of soul, were not our speakers and newspapers so enslaved to the vulgar habit as to boast ten times of the thousands of square miles it covered with armed men, for once that they alluded to the motive that gave it all its meaning and splendour?' Perhaps that phrase of the 'unrivalled stress of soul' was itself somewhat in the expansive aquiline taste; but the corrective thought is medicinal; and never more so than to-day, when not a few Americans find in the prospect of extra-American empire a welcome fillip to the kind of imagination that had been jaded by too much rhetoric in the key that Lowell

Patriotism and Militarism

deprecated. It has come to this, that republicans are acclaiming the principle of 'empire' in modern Boston as eagerly as they ever did in ancient Athens, and that citizens of the vast United States are seriously insisting on their national need for 'expansion.'

It cannot be too plainly said that if, as many Americans seriously argue, their economic life needs such expansion—if the acquisition of Cuba is necessitated by the mere exhaustion of the field of profitable investment in the States—the game of democratic politics so far is up. No European State has failed more completely to place its industrial life on a sound basis that the States must be held to have done if that theorem be sound. If there is a positive need in American affairs for expansion of territory, Cuba and the Philippines can but stave off the evil day, and the industrial failure of the Republic is only a question of time. And to whom is that conclusion credible?

It is doubtless only too true that a number of persons in the States may count on enriching themselves by the annexation of new territory; but that their pecuniary gain should count as the moral and political gain of the Republic; and that the future of the commonwealth should be held to turn on such chronic expansion of its realm—this is, if possible, worse doctrine than the gospel of Mr. Henley. Yet when professed Liberals and professed haters of Liberalism in England are found at one in egging on the new imperialists of the Republic, it is not beyond the bounds of chance that the mania may gather head. For the people of the States, albeit they are no more 'Anglo-Saxon' than the motley population which hypnotizes itself with that shibboleth in the mother-country, are subject to all the visitations of unwisdom which follow the rest of mankind, Britons included. Only their special circumstances have spared them certain phases in the past; and now that they are suddenly placed in a new relation, reason must in that connection fight for its own hand there as elsewhere. There is no treasure of surplus sanity in the life of a republic any more than in that of a monarchy. The Spanish war has been taken in the States just as wars are taken in Europe —a matter to be specially considered anon— and only a minority combats the new pride of conquest. Unhappily, there is old as well as new counsel in its favour; for Lowell, of all men, can be cited on the militarist side. 'We have at length established,' he wrote a generation ago, 'our claim to the noblesse of the sword, the first step still of every nation that would make its entry into the best society of

Patriotism and Militarism 63

history.' The *premier pas* in that case certainly cost a good deal; and it would appear to follow that it is good business to take a few more, till the States have all the evidence of noblesse they want, and constitute as good society as Turkey itself. When the patriot author of the *Biglow Papers* can be cited to such purpose, it is not strange, though it be sad, that some of his successors in American letters should now be found looking to military patriotism for the sufficient inspiration of a truly American literature. The blood of the volunteers, it seems, is to be the seed of a new literary church. Says one of that persuasion, in an essay of which I have seen an extract:

> 'When American life has become a unit in its moral and spiritual aspiration, when local pride is swallowed up in national pride, the American soil will be ready to produce the great art, the great book. Until then no one can speak for America as Homer spoke for Greece, Shakespeare for England, Dante for Italy.'

Never was the judicial warning against giving reasons for a judgment more pat than here. What would otherwise be mere intangible declamation, open to blame but outside argument, is delivered into our hands as false history, false æsthetics, false sociology. For Homer did not 'speak for Greece,' nor Shakespeare for 'England,' nor Dante for 'Italy.'

64 Patriotism and Empire

The Homeric epics, fruits of a life that was hardly even an embryo of the Greece of the world's memory, no more speak for civilized Greece than does the *Chanson de Roland* for France, or the *Nibelungenlied* for Germany; and Hawthorne already has 'spoken for America,' in so far as that may be, much more truly than Homer could possibly do for the Greece of Pericles, or Shakespeare for modern England. The vanity of the theorem is flagrant when we remember that long after Homer Greece was divided into a multitude of States; that most of the best of later Greek literature was produced by Athens alone; and that Dante stood for one Italian faction in one Italian city—a faction at chronic war with its rival, a city at chronic war with its nearest neighbour. Did the great Greek tragedians speak for Sparta? or Plato for Thrace? or Sappho for Bœotia? Dante did not even dream of a federated Italy: his allegiance was to an empire seated on alien soil. The dream was dreamed by Machiavelli, who might indeed be said to speak for the Italy of his day; but Italy in our own age has been united for a generation, and Leopardi still remains her greatest modern man of letters.

Union, verily, is better than strife, and cosmopolitanism than provincialism; but mere

Patriotism and Militarism 65

communal pride is not cosmopolitanism, not if it be stretched to cover a hundred millions of souls; and so stretched it has less virtue for literature than has Mireio's love for Provence. It was not pride in Scotland that made Burns a lyrist and a rustic Aristophanes; there have been millions of Bruce-worshippers and thistle-flourishers since his day, whose nationalism has only put them the further from great art. Nor was it in the least degree any pride in England, or any unity of aspiration with his fellows, that made Shakespeare what he was. His patriotic period is the period of his first-fruits; and to pretend that he 'speaks for England' in *Hamlet* and *Lear* and *Othello*, is to invert the whole lesson of literary things. One had supposed that it was adjudged his supreme attainment to have spoken 'not for an age, but for all time,' not for a nation but for humanity, as did Sappho and Omar Khayyam, in whom we trace not a vestige of a national consciousness.

This theme is worth thrashing out here and now, on whatsoever provocation. The doctrine that national pride yields literature of which nations may be proud is an error of errors, a falsity of falsities. It has some touch of primary colour from the case of Virgil; but the deification of Augustus and the thrill of pride over Rome's mock-mission,

'Parcere subjectis et debellare superbos,'

did not make Virgil a greater poet than the cosmopolitan and even didactic Lucretius, nor lend the vibrant note of the pre-Augustan and wayward Catullus to imperialistic Horace. Far be it from me to fall back on the formula that the spirit of genius bloweth whither it listeth. Rather, it blows where it can; and the very point of the issue is, that neither nationalism nor provincialism, neither local nor continental patriotism, as such, constitutes any favouring soil for genius in the lack of the true sociological conditions; that, on the contrary, megalomaniacal and parochial patriotism alike are in themselves noxious to great art.

It is noteworthy that our theorist did not add 'Goethe for Germany' to his examples. The rebound of the idea would have been too jarring to his case. Goethe and Schiller and Herder at Weimar spoke, in their degrees, not for Germany but for the civilized world; and though Goethe did in the Napoleonic time wince at German subjection, and did later aspire to a political union of Germany, he owed his literary output to no patriotic inspiration, and expressly protested against the idea of a centralized German Empire. Such an empire, or something tending that way, has come, and where now are the Goethes, the Schillers, the Heines? Sir Robert Morier well said of Bismarck, that he had made Germany great, but made small the German. It is the bald fact that, in well-nigh a generation of German pride in German unity, we have seen not one great German book, to speak either 'for' Germany, or to Europe. The vaunted charm has failed utterly. Goethe it was who said that the time has gone by for national literatures, and that the literature of the future must be cosmopolitan. Behold the strict fulfilment of his speech!

It is indeed an express dishonour to literature to define it as being at its best an utterance or outcome of that one of all the animal instincts which has been the least sublimated in civilized life. In contrast with the passion of love, the passion of hate, on all its lines, remains nudely barbarian; and the false fraternity that grafts on it is ethically the very lowest form of the spirit of union. Not by voicing such elementary emotions has literature come to be a spring of moral sustenance and joy to men. In the oldest of the great epopees known to us, the highest moments are manifestly those in which the singer transcends the blinder passions of the earlier prime, and looks from a height of grave compassion on the clashing destinies of men. Not the rage and triumph of Achilles, but the trouble and the doom of Hector, Andromache's penalty and Priam's pain, make noble for all time the poems we call by the name of Homer. Not the well-lost war-songs of Tyrtæus, but the manifold sympathy of the tragic drama and the brooding of the thinkers, lift Greek literature on high for the later nations. To think of Dante and Montaigne, Cervantes and Shakespeare and Goethe, Hawthorne and Leopardi, as instruments to the very passion which would most meanly circumscribe their realm, and most utterly turn to naught their best desires, is to blaspheme their genius. The spirit of considerate speech was not evolved to be 'procuress to the lords of hell.'

Let a bellicose patriotism qualify for supreme literary renown, and literature is already lowered to the level of the military band. Nothing, indeed, is more intelligible in current culture-evolution among us than the concurrence of patriotism and imperialism in the ethic, with gory sensationalism in the subject-matter, of the prevailing type of fiction. Not subtlety, but stimulation; not character, but adventure; not psychology, but the shedding of blood; not thought, but bustle and excitement, are the requirements to-day met by two English

Patriotism and Militarism 69

fictionists out of three. The prime favourite is Mr. Kipling, the best of whose later work is fatally withheld from greatness by the now inveterate intrusion of swagger—a spirit destructive of all artistic sincerity and devotion—in his every mental process, artistic or other; and in such well-knit rhetoric as his *Recessional*, a patriotic public takes its devout delight as whole-heartedly as it appreciated the nod and wink of the *Departmental Ditties* and the jovial chorussing of the *Barrack-Room Ballads*. The theology is strictly worthy of the sociology. In the *Recessional*, the patriot intones the lesson that, since pride goeth before a fall, we do well to assure Omnipotence that we are not proud. It wants little that we offer up sacrifices of propitiation. For less ceremonial purposes, we figure for ourselves in the rest of the new gospel as the Dominant Race, beside whom Baboos, Home Rulers, and Russians, are as creeping things. And it is all very good. The literary palate of patriotism suits with its philosophy and ethic. Even in the rank rodomontade of the *Song of the Sword*, Mr. Henley is too much of an artist for the maws he fain would glut; but he and the rest of the patriotic elect find their fit sociologist in the painter of *The Gadsbys;* as Dickens is still their ideal of a true novelist. Which things are an allegory.

But such thoughts are by the way. It is enough here to insist that, when the artist would preach and the lyrist lead, they are presuming on their place, and can no more yield us great counsel than great art. Not by the children of instinct and impulse shall the knot of a great destiny be untied for mankind; not from schoolboy fervours and vulgar heats shall come the inspiration of a literature worthy of a fully charted world. Let the lyrist, if he will, sing his heats and hates, as he does his loves and sorrows; but let him not think for that to rank, and let not those think to stand as thinkers who rank him, with either the trusted leaders or the pedestalled light-givers of mankind. He has chosen his function, and his place is assigned by the laws of an evolution above his grasp.

PART II

The Militarist Regimen

I

FROM the same animal roots with patriotism, we have seen, spring the proclivities which in these days we mark by the names of militarism and imperialism. Hence their prosperity. The enormous waste of treasure and power which now proceeds continuously in the armaments of the European nations could never have been undertaken, and could still less be maintained, on any mere calculation of necessity such as is habitually alleged in defence of each country's expenditure. The impulse roots in malice, passion, and pride. It is no genuine apprehension of attack that prompts the successive efforts of all the leading States to exceed or overtake each other's armaments. In so far as panics are not set up — as so often among ourselves — by the deliberate strategy of the militarist interest and the special industrial interests which depend on militarism, the sufficient motive is the blind instinct to attain the complacency of power by equality in its display. Nations compete in that display very much as do parvenus in their equipages. Each nation normally professes to suspect offensive purposes on the part of its neighbours, while repudiating any such purpose on its own part; but when the forms of peaceful intercourse tend to force a choice between an avowal of universal hypocrisy and one of universal folly, the average militarist, shifting his ground, undertakes to make out that the institution of armaments is a good thing in itself. From the defence of armaments to the panegyric of war is but a step, and we have had an abundance of both within the past year, as a result of the sudden eirenicon of the Tsar of Russia.

The *locus classicus* of such doctrinaires is the saying of Moltke, to the effect that the hope of universal peace is a dream, 'and not even a beautiful dream.' Moltke was indeed a precious authority on beautiful dreams; and the record of his rage at the swift recuperation of France while Germany was plunged in industrial depression through her very receipt of the French indemnity, is the never-to-be-forgotten measure of his political wisdom. He was eager, his

The Militarist Regimen 73

own countrymen tell us, to pick a quarrel by way of striking a new and more ruinous blow at the neighbouring State. When such minds can rank as oracles and framers of ideals for bodies of civilized men, how far are we raised above the ethics and the sociology of savages?

That the gospel of Moltke is a good hearing to many among us may be gathered from a whole handful of review articles of the past twelve months. Gentlemen whose ostensible qualifications for political counsel are military and other titles, and who are palpably incompetent to conduct any argument coherently for three consecutive steps, have informed us of their contempt for the understandings of those who cherish hopes of any measure of proportional disarmament. Instead, however, of reciprocating contempt with such reasoners, let us follow closely for a moment the reasoning of one writer, presumably competent from the militarist standpoint, who as an experienced journalist represents a good deal of public opinion.

War, according to this writer, is a form of evil that in time must pass away. 'A period will come,' he predicts, 'when militarism will appear as unnatural as slavery now appears to ourselves.'* He is at the same time satisfied,

---

* Article, 'Should Europe Disarm?' by Sidney Low, in *Nineteenth Century*, October, 1898.

however, that, 'at least in our time,' it is not an evil but a good, and he urges a variety of reasons why we should cherish it. 'No people has risen to greatness without its discipline; few have been able to develop the highest excellence in art, science, learning, or industry, except under its impulse. The great literary ages are usually those which have followed upon successful war. . . . The age of Pericles was not one in which men knew nothing of fighting, nor was the age of Dante, nor the age of Elizabeth.' The thesis is not new, and it may be worth while to consider it. At the outset it may be noted that if for 'fighting' and 'war' we substituted 'pestilence,' or 'cruelty,' or 'baseness,' the proposition would be equally plausible. As there never has been a historic age in which men 'knew nothing of fighting,' the special connection of such knowledge with the ages of Pericles and Dante and Elizabeth is a species of sophism that merely impeaches its framer. Could he show that great literary and artistic and scientific movements always concurred with special stresses of war, he would go far to prove his case; but no such thesis can be sustained. Could he show, on the other hand, that movements of the kind under notice always occur immediately after special stresses of war, and that wars always

The Militarist Regimen 75

have such a sequel, though he would leave open the inference that they stood for disgust of war, he would be at least supporting the claim that war somehow promoted intellectual life. But he does not even attempt to prove this, and, as a matter of fact, such a statement would be wildly untrue. The section of ancient Greece which paid most zealous heed to the business of war throughout its whole history was Sparta, of all Hellenic States the most utterly devoid of art, letters, and philosophy. The reigns of Henry VII. and Henry VIII. in England followed upon a long period of desperate civil war; but they were not distinguished by any great literary or artistic developments. The renascence began in the reign of Elizabeth long before the Armada, and that episode can in no intelligible way be causally connected with the performance of Spenser, Shakespeare, and Bacon. Germany was soon afterwards plunged in a war that lasted thirty years, and German literature and science well-nigh disappeared. In later France, literature and science, vigorous at the accession of Louis XIV., fell away during the period of his successful wars, revived after the disasters of the closing years of his reign, flourished greatly during generations in which the nation lost much and gained little by war, were eclipsed during the period of Napoleon, recovered after his overthrow, and since the greater overthrow of Sedan have been as vigorous as ever. Modern English literature is presumably to be held as flourishing in the hands of Tennyson, Browning, Arnold, Thackeray, and science in the hands of Darwin. Is such florescence, then, to be attributed to the wretched episode of the Crimea, the one considerable English war between Waterloo and our own day? Germany has produced not one great imaginative writer of European importance since Heine. Behold the efficacy of the successful wars of 1866 and 1870! From warless Scandinavia we have Ibsen; Russia, after the Crimea, produces the great fiction of Tourguenief, Tolstoy, Dostoyevsky. If successful militarism be the secret, why does not Germany do as much? Why did not the great period of American literature follow instead of preceding the Civil War? And why, again, did not Latin literature revive under Trajan or Severus, or at any other point in the career of chronic military success between the generation of Augustus and the fourth century?

The theorem, in fine, is an absolute fallacy: it misses real causes and suggests unreal. But

The Militarist Regimen

the militarist, swinging at random between the eulogy of war and its deprecation, can shift to the other leg, and argue that 'the great armaments do not tend to promote war, but the contrary.' Recollecting that in that case they are thwarting what he has described as a great civilizing force, he hastily adds that, after all, they do not prevent war: 'the rare and brief, if terrible, wars of modern times will supply that occasional tonic of which the body politic stands in need.' But then, again, armaments are a tonic even without war. 'Meanwhile, the careful and systematic preparation for the possible conflict is an invaluable discipline which seems'—only seems, though invaluable—'to be required in an age when comfort is growing, and religion'—alas! with all the discipline—'is losing its power to lift the spirits of men above a grovelling materialism!' So we are to get back to the spirituality of Dugald Dalgetty by the way of the barrack and the machine-gun.

On this theme our militarist waxes eloquent. 'The Cobdenite ideal of a State in which every citizen is ceaselessly engaged in the ennobling process of buying cheap and selling dear leaves something to be desired. The accumulation of riches, and the steady pursuit of material comfort, do not tend to the development of the highest type of character.' Is the militarist, then, as a rule concerned to substitute a higher structure of civic life for that which he thinks fit to associate with the name of Richard Cobden, who deplored it? Yearnings he would seem to have, not in his own natural kind. 'Before we abolish the soldier on economic grounds, we had better arrange for the diffusion as well as the increase of wealth.' Most true; how, then, shall we begin? Suppose we sketch a programme of Old Age Pensions, of nationalization, first of land, then of railways, then of other industries, shall we have the militarist's support? Or has he another scheme of his own? He speaks sympathetically of Tommy Atkins as so much better housed than his civilian brothers; and of the conscription in Germany as a 'continuation school for the people, for which we have no substitute in this country.' Will the militarist vote, then, be cast for a measure that aims at raising the whole level of elementary education, and rebuilding our industrial cities? It is unpleasant to have to say it; but there is not a shadow of ground for believing that the flourish about the diffusion of wealth and comfort and culture is aught but a device to disparage peace and peaceful life, to the end, not of mending the latter, but of maintaining the regimen of

The Militarist Regimen 79

the sword. The 'highest type of character' is to be formed not otherwise than by training the helots of labour to disembowel dervishes. 'The precision, the drilled alertness, and the ready obedience of the men,' as seen in German ironworks, 'are the qualities fostered by intelligent military training.' What now becomes of the disparagement of the competitive industrial life, if armies are actually to be encouraged by way of quickening the industrial pace? And what, again, becomes of the fling against the Cobdenite ideal, when the theorist meets the difficulty as to the poverty of Italy and Russia by saying that they 'are, in any case, miserably poor countries'? 'They have great natural resources which have remained undeveloped owing to the lack of capital and want of efficient industrial enterprise.' In this convenient fashion, zealous commercialism figures as an evil to be moderated by military expenditure; and the countries which suffer from their military expenditure are told that their real trouble is lack of zealous commercialism. To cast out the Cobdenite ideal, you are to set up an army; to pay for an army, you are to set up the Cobdenite ideal.

Continuing his appeal to his formerly flouted Cobdenite, our sociologist argues that 'if a conscription would *restore* to the English working man that superiority in the habits of order, discipline, and steady industry which he seems to be *yielding* to his foreign competitors, it would be worth the cost.' It would thus appear that the conscript countries have out-Cobdened that Cobdenite ideal which conscription was to resist; they are beating us, if not at selling dear, at least at selling. But, on the other hand, it is implied that undrilled English workmen *had* the superiority in question, without any training, at a time when their rivals had the same military training as now. How, then, did they attain it; and why should they not retain it without conscription?

Coming to the simple question of fact, we are speedily compelled to note that in so far as England is suffering from competition in the iron trade, her successful rivals are not the militarist nations but the United States, and that rapid developments of machinery count for a great deal more in the matter than any training of the workers. We are thus left inquiring with some emphasis whether the militarist case has anything behind it but reciprocally annihilative sophisms. The dissertation before us yields nothing else, unless it be the romantic appeal for a restoration of the power of religion ' to lift the spirits of men above a grovelling materialism;' and here we are faced by the fatality that there is rather more professed materialism in Russia, Germany, France, and Italy than in either England or the United States. It may seem brutal thus to follow up an amiable sentimentalist with logical tests ; but on his own principles strife is a noble and elevating thing ; and we must even strive bloodlessly when the other method is closed. And as our militarist is clearly not developing towards precision and drilled alertness of the understanding, we can but credit him, finally, with pleading in the old way for the so-called military virtues—precision, that is, not in the use of productive tools, for that would merely realize the Cobdenite ideal, but in shooting ; drilled alertness, not of the mind, but of the body, for the due promotion of spirituality ; and the ready obedience of horses and dogs to an outside will. *Sic itur ad astra.*

II

If such self-stultifying advocacy as this were employed on behalf of any good or humane cause, with what derision would it not be greeted! and to what deliquescence of 'sentimentalism' would it not be held to point! By sentimentalism we all mean, I suppose, a kind of dreaming which confuses fact with fancy, wishes with happenings; but that there is a barbarian as well as a civilized sentimentalism is a truth necessarily hidden from the would-be wise and prudent barbarian, though it may be discerned by the babes and sucklings of social science. Men with a taste for armaments, piqued by censure, determine to follow their bent, incidentally going about to offer us estimates of the good effects of militarism on life; and all the while they are much further from a judicial estimate than the most fanatical devotee of peace, who really takes into account the larger mass of social phenomena. In all the militarist literature of the subject, German, French, or English, you may look in vain for anything more philosophical than a German paralogism about surplus energy, a French truism about the naturalness of strife,* or an English falsism, such as that we have been examining, about the sequence of literary movements upon periods of war. The most circumspect men on that side are driven back on an *ignoratio elenchi* when they would reason. Take, for instance, a passage in which one of

* The most strenuous exposition of that theme, however, is the English *Philosophy of War* of Mr. James Ram (1878), a work chiefly fitted to encourage every human being to do whatever ill he pleases, on the score that Nature is always so employed.

The Militarist Regimen

the most esteemed of modern expert writers on warfare, Captain Mahan, recently professes to balance the pros and cons of the issue :

'On the economical side there is the diminution of production, the tax upon men's time and lives, the disadvantages or evils so dinned daily into our ears that there is no need of repeating them here. But is there nothing to the credit side of the account, even perhaps a balance in their favour? Is it nothing, in an age when authority is weakening and restraints are loosening, that the youth of a nation passes through a school in which order, obedience, and reverence are learned, where the body is systematically developed, where ideals of self-surrender, of courage, of manhood, are inculcated, necessarily, because fundamental conditions of military success? Is it nothing that masses of youths out of the fields and streets are brought together, mingled with others of higher intellectual antecedents, taught to work and to act together, mind in contact with mind, and carrying back into civil life that respect for constituted authority which is urgently needed in these days when lawlessness is erected into a religion? It is a suggestive lesson to watch the expression and movements of a number of rustic conscripts undergoing their first drills, and to contrast them with the finished result as seen in the faces and bearing of the soldiers that throng the streets. A military training is not the worst preparation for an active life, any more than the years spent at college are time lost, as another school of utilitarians insists. Is it nothing that wars are less frequent, peace better secured, by the mutual respect of nations for each other's strength; and that, when a convulsion does come, it passes rapidly, leaving the ordinary course of events to resume sooner, and therefore more easily? War now not only occurs more rarely, but has rather the character of an occasional excess, from

Patriotism and Empire

which recovery is easy. A century or more ago it was a chronic disease. And withal, the military spirit, the preparedness—not merely the willingness, which is a different thing—to fight in a good cause, which is a distinct good, is more widely diffused and more thoroughly possessed than ever it was when the soldier was merely the paid man. It is the nations now that are in arms, and not simply the servants of the King.'

In a previous page of the same volume, Captain Mahan had laid stress on the danger to our civilization from barbarians who are 'wholly alien' to its spirit, and on the absolute necessity, in this regard, of the 'attitude of armed watchfulness between nations' in Europe; but in the passage before us he waives that alleged necessity, which, if real, might be supposed to supersede any other justification for armaments, and considers rather the risk from 'barbarians within,' by which expression he apparently means Socialists. The gallant author's conception of controversy may pass undiscussed, but not so his professional theory of social discipline. If militarists choose to meddle with sociology, they must bide the test, and this is how Captain Mahan's theorem works out on analysis :

1. Militarism is of value as an efficient training for war; and as such it involves the learning of order, obedience, and reverence, which are valuable to-day, when, with so much

The Militarist Regimen

less of war than formerly, 'authority is loosening and restraints are weakening.'

2. But war, all the same, is a disease, and last century it was 'a chronic disease.' The state of health is that in which you so carefully qualify yourself for the state of disease that you are unprecedentedly fitted to catch it, but do not. At the same time, while thus healthy, thus unprecedentedly prepared to fight 'in a good cause,' the 'nations in arms' exhibit the social phenomena of weakening authority and loosening restraints, and 'lawlessness is erected into a religion.' So that the law-abiding and orderly ages were the chronically diseased ages, and a training for the nations in reverence and obedience coincides with a maximum of systematic lawlessness.

This is a synthesis of Captain Mahan's own propositions, so made as to show their logical relation. If men in general were wont to discard self-contradiction from their life-philosophy as they discard it from matters of business and machinery, there would be no need to do more. Since, however, logically false positions are not taken up on any logical impulse, but stand for false foregone convictions, the reader so placed is not likely to be shaken by the mere exposure of his inconsistency. It is therefore incumbent on the opposition to fight out the case on the points of fact.

The passage under notice asserts, implicitly or explicitly, the following things :

1. Men of little education trained together with more educated men in camps for war, with or without actual war, acquire a respect for constituted authority.

2. A military training is a good preparation for civic life.

3. Under a system of general conscription, the nations acquire a 'mutual respect for each other's strength,' which makes war rarer than formerly, when 'the soldier was merely the paid man.' It also passes more quickly.

We have only to compare these propositions with the historical facts to see that they are all astray. In nearly all the leading European States where conscription exists, it is notorious that the training camp serves as a school for Socialism, which develops a deep disrespect for authority as at present constituted. Hear the view of a conservative French politician, M. Delafosse :

'I consider obligatory military service, as it exists among us, the worst agent of social disintegration and national desolation. I am convinced that, if we permit it to continue the ravages which it has already begun to produce, in twenty years there will be no more society, no more

The Militarist Regimen 87

army, nothing but the dust of a people, without bond or cohesion. . . . From a social point of view, the effects produced by obligatory military service, as we know it, are infinitely perilous to the future of society. It produces a rupture of equilibrium which is one of the great dangers of the present hour, and I consider obligatory military service as one of the most powerful agents of revolutionary Socialism."*

It may be that M. Delafosse, in his fear of Socialism, which he shares with Captain Mahan, puts a false face on the tendency even of the revolutionary form : that is for the anti-Socialist militarist to discuss. To promote Socialism, as apart from revolution, is in the eyes of the rest of us no discredit to barrack life, but, at all events, the fact is the reverse of Captain Mahan's proposition. What is no less to the purpose is the fact that in previous ages camp life has made men at once amenable to the rule of their general and potentially careless of other constituted authority when that happened to clash with his. The legions of Cæsar learned no reverence for the State, and as little did the troopers of Cromwell, who at his beck overthrew the Parliament under whose authority they had drawn the sword. The lesson is one worth recalling by the democratic politics of to-day. It is assumed, at Captain Mahan's

* Cited in ' Can We Disarm ?' by Joseph McCabe and Georges Darrien. Heinemann, 1899.

point of view, that we can all be armed to the teeth, drilled to the toes, and constantly prepared to fight 'in a good cause'—as if any nation ever went to war feeling the cause was bad—without coming to blows save by way of 'occasional excess,' though it is simply inconceivable that men would go on drilling for a hundred years if the 'occasional excess' did not come as 'chronic disease' to make the preparation relevant. And, as a matter of fact, war between the nations is not controlled or determined by the mere practice of conscription, as Captain Mahan asserts.

In ancient Greece and Italy, military training was universal, and before the supremacy of Rome war was yet a 'chronic disease.' In the post-Norman period, military training was universal in England and Scotland, and their wars were chronic down till the middle of the sixteenth century, nor did the same conditions avert three invasions of France by England between 1339 and 1415. It is true that Cromwell speedily turned the instrument of a standing army and navy to the account of wilful war; but the decline thereafter of the practice of general military training was not, any more than in the period of Elizabeth and James I., coincident with more war than had gone on in the days of general militarism. It

The Militarist Regimen 89

is true, again—and let Captain Mahan's compatriots note the circumstance—that a paid army is more readily available for expeditions against weaker States than would be a purely conscript force ; but mere conscription does not discredit war. Napoleon's wars were made with conscript troops, and modern Europe has seen the Austro-French, the Crimean, the Austro-Prussian, the Franco-German, and the Russo-Turkish wars within one generation, a record certainly not surpassed in the previous century. As to the brevity of modern wars, it has nothing to do with the general bearing of arms by the nations. The Peloponnesian war lasted twenty-seven years, and it followed on a thirty years' peace. On the other hand, the American Civil War was brought to an end by the inequality of the combatants in resources. If a modern war between well-matched States should end speedily, it would not be because of their fitness for fighting, but because the war was so rapidly ruinous, or because men now come more rapidly to reason—a point calling for more attention than militarists care to give it.

If since 1880 the great nations have visibly shrunk from anything like equal war, it is from sheer rational perception of the horror and the insanity of the course for which all militarism is a preparation. It is not a 'mutual respect' so much as simple knowledge and reflection thereon. France and Germany know that if they grapple again, both will 'bleed as white as veal.' The rulers of Russia know that war with any first-rate Power may bring the autocracy to bankruptcy and ruin. But who will predict that no fortuitous Armageddon shall come of the competing rapacities of the European nations in China and Africa?

Supposing it be otherwise: supposing a whole generation to pass without the firing of another shot by land or sea between civilized peoples, our children will be very definitely faced—unless, indeed, it is progressively solved in the interim—by the problem, Is it worth the while of civilized States to go on drilling men for wars that are seen to be avoidable? From Captain Mahan's point of view, the answer should be Yes. Camp drill, he argues, is a good preparation for civic life. Now, it is *a priori* inconceivable that training for an extinct function can in perpetuity be the best preparation for a real function; and in so far as the plea for drill is merely a plea for bodily training, the obvious answer is that where that is seen to have been generally neglected the nations can perfectly well provide for it without any pretence of military drill. If undrilled rustics

The Militarist Regimen

and mechanics are inferior in grace and activity to drilled soldiers, these, on the other hand, are not superior to undrilled gentlemen. The point hardly bears discussing. To urge drill as the only feasible means to the physical education of rustics and artisans is to imply that there is no hope of a vital betterment in the lot of rustics and artisans as such. But the very suggestion elicits the remembrance that through the ages grinding toil for the poor has been the fixed correlative of militarism. And the conclusion that begins to emerge for us is that the science which should solve the social problem is not only never furthered, but forever frustrated of growth, if not denied bare birth, by the survival of the militarist ideal and practice. Against the facile claim that military training is a good preparative for civic life there lies the tacit testimony of the whole history of civilization, scientifically considered. We who gainsay militarism desire nothing more than the hearing of the issue.

III

It would be pedantic, perhaps, to set out with much insistence on the fact that the higher or non-barbarian civilization historically *begins* with communities in which the trade of the soldier is specialized, as in ancient Egypt, and whole classes are entirely withdrawn from military service. It could still be answered that Æschylus and Socrates bore arms, who were of more value than many Egyptians; and though it is sociologically clear that the Greek civilization, with its rule of military service for all citizens, could never have flourished as it did but for the seeds of culture it drew from those of Egypt and Asia, the question thus far remains open as between the advocates of normal militarism and us who oppose them. Let us, then, seek in the higher civilizations themselves for the decisive data.

As between the different States of Greece, there was diversity of devotion to the military life, Sparta marking the acme of the cult, Athens a more moderate passion. 'We do not afflict ourselves with laborious training,' claimed Pericles; 'and yet, in the hour of trial, our courage does not fail . . .; we are as ready for action as those who spend their lives in anticipating danger and preparing to meet it. So much the greater is our gain.' What the modern militarist will say on the matter we need hardly consider; he will scarcely seek to exalt the barren and mindless militarism of Sparta over the immeasurably richer life of Athens; though, on the militarist theory, the

The Militarist Regimen 93

Spartan should be the greater civilization. But supposing him to claim Athens as his golden mean, let him show us wherein her measure of militarism fitted her citizens the better for anything but the fighting themselves provoked. For what civil functions were her epheboi and her marines prepared? Not for wise decisions in policy; not for clearer thought in ethics; not for closer industry; not for finer art. It was after their maximum of military experience, gained in the ruinous Peloponnesian war, that their civic polity decayed past cure. A generation of venomous war had broken down alike respect for constituted authority and belief in a moral law; till hatred had eaten up reason, and war only ceased because of sheer loss of blood. It is well to recall the judgment of Thucydides on the temper bred by the war throughout Greece:

'When troubles had once begun in the cities, those who followed carried the revolutionary spirit further and further, and determined to outdo the report of all who had preceded them, by the ingenuity of their enterprises and the atrocity of their revenges. The meaning of words had no longer the same relation to things, but were changed by them as they thought proper. Reckless daring was held to be loyal courage; prudent delay was the excuse of a coward; moderation was the disguise of unmanly weakness; to know everything was to do nothing. Frantic energy was the true quality of a man . . . the lover of violence was always trusted, and his opponent suspected. . . . He who plotted from the first to have nothing to do with plots was a breaker-up of parties and a poltroon who was afraid of the enemy. In a word, he who could outstrip another in a bad action was applauded; and so was he who encouraged to evil one who had no idea of it. . . . Revenge was dearer than self-preservation. Any agreements sworn to by either party, when they could do nothing else, were binding just as long as they were powerless. . . . Striving in every way to overcome each other, they committed the most monstrous crimes; yet even these were surpassed by the magnitude of their revenges. . . . Thus revolution gave birth to every form of wickedness in Hellas. The simplicity which is so large an element in a noble nature was laughed to scorn and disappeared. An attitude of perfidious antagonism everywhere prevailed; for there was no word binding enough nor oath terrible enough to reconcile enemies. . . . Inferior intellects generally succeeded best.'

Such was the 'type of character' moulded by a generation of war in the highest civilization of the ancient world, a land of democracies, in which all citizens were trained to arms. A better case for war could doubtless be made out by taking the armies of later imperial Rome, and looking only at the better types shaped by them, the steadfast centurions, the magnanimous generals like Agricola. But that was precisely the sort of army that Captain Mahan disparages, the army in which the soldier was only the paid man. And, indeed, the common soldier in them was made at best but a tough veteran, a

The Militarist Regimen 95

stout gladiator. Still, it is hard to see his moral inferiority to the men of the earlier ages, who fought for Rome against the liberties of every other Italian State, till at length the totality of acquired faculty for civic life made possible an inferno of domestic butchery, Sulla outdoing the massacres of Marius, till the republic swooned into peace, and grew fit for the rule of the autocrat.

To get a justified opinion on the value of militarism as a training for civic tasks, we may either follow the general fortunes of any one of the military empires of antiquity, or study the great captains in their civic capacities. Any other method must fall more or less short of rational investigation. Now, every ancient military State or empire of which we possess the history does but present a story of more or less rapid decadence. The seven successive Oriental empires, the minor 'empires' of Athens and Sparta, the Empire of Alexander and his successors, that of Rome, those of her conquerors, those of the Saracens, are so many colossal proofs that the life of arms never taught to any the secret of stable evolution. The Eastern Roman Empire, with a standing army and no militia, did indeed subsist precariously for a thousand years ; but the measure of militarism which so far preserved it availed not a jot for progress in the arts or the science of civic life. A system of conscription would only have multiplied and worsened the risks of inner strife. Machiavelli in later Italy, weary of *condottieri*, pined for a return to the militarism of republican Rome; but that could only have led to a different species of subjection from what actually befel, the empire of a Borgia rather than the empire of Spain. It was the universal soldiering of the earlier Italian republics that led to the mercenary armies of the later. The law of all militarism, on the face of all history, is a law of decay.

And the lesson is, if possible, still clearer when we consider the great commanders as politicians. In the ancient world, Alexander, Hannibal, and Cæsar were the greatest of the great; and each and all were as powerless to build up a durable polity as they were potent to overthrow. Alexander's empire was a political impossibility, momentarily made by a convulsion of conquest; its speedy disruption was as inevitable as any process of nature. The iron will and inhuman vigilance of Hannibal could maintain him with his alien host in hostile Italy for fifteen years; he could manœuvre a Roman host into a pen and slay them like sheep; but he could not cure the corroding civic malady of Carthage; nor was

The Militarist Regimen

the mighty Julius a whit more gifted for the healing of the cancer of Rome. He could but ruin a republic, to make way for an empire that fatally progressed to a ruin immeasurably greater.

Here and there we may indeed find a worthy captain, who could lead in war and shine in peace. Timoleon and Alfred are noble names. But such men do not test the issue : they were warriors against their will ; champions of struggling causes, not representatives of the militarist ideal ; nor is there any reason to regard them as deep-seeing statesmen, though they won an honourable fame. The strict type of military genius is Cromwell, who, by the admission of his latest historian, to say nothing of the plain facts of history, could only wield force, and was impotent to plan a continuing State. Of all great modern soldiers, Frederick and Napoleon show most of faculty for civic rule. But Frederick, the successful ruler of the two, came to hate the life of war, whose arts he had had painfully to learn ; nor did even he build a polity that could of itself stand firm after him ; while Napoleon's ruling hand stifled thought and speech as effectively as it stimulated lower activities, and his empire fell as swiftly as it rose ; even as a generation served to bring Frederick's iron machine to rust and wreck.

Washington was more liberally wise; but he was no heaven-born soldier or lover of camps; and it is very significant for us in this connection that the military element has never once counted for good in American statesmanship. The first typical soldier in the Presidential chair was Andrew Jackson, from whose Presidency dates the system of spoils of office. Of all modern soldiers, one of the most estimable as a man was General Grant; but it is confessed by his own party that he managed ill as President. War had not fitted *him* for civil life, with all his patience and integrity. It is indeed said of Lincoln, I doubt not with perfect justice, that he showed an admirable judgment in military matters, and was positively superior to most of his generals. But that is only saying that a masterly statesman may judge sagaciously of plans of warfare; it is no proof that a training in actual warfare would even have left him the masterly statesman he was. Lincoln was prepared by a purely civic life for a colossal civic problem, which included a military problem: the man demonstrably prepared for a great civic problem by a military life is still to seek.

Our own Wellington is almost, if not quite, the negation of the needed instance. He had wisdom enough — and perhaps some non-military statesman in his place might have shown less — avowedly to yield to political pressure rather than provoke civil war; but of guiding or constructive faculty he does not seem to have shown a glimmer. The measure of his independent civic wisdom is his protest against facilities to third-class railway passengers, on the score that they were 'a premium to the lower orders to go uselessly wandering about the country.' Such maxims do we receive from the victor of Waterloo. And of Nelson, noting what is on record as to his political intelligence, and his personality as apart from his genius, we may gravely say that he was fortunate, and we no less so, in the time of his death. With his tyrannous proclivities, his prestige, and his grievous lack of human wisdom, he would have become, had he survived Trafalgar, one of the most dangerous political forces in English life.

Wellington, who by chance met and judged him, and who was so far superior to him in the faculty of personal balance, leaves little doubt as to the great seaman's want of sense as a man. They met, as the well-known narrative of the Duke runs, in the Colonial Office:

'He [Nelson] could not know who I was; but he entered at once into conversation with me, if I can call it conversation, for it was almost all on his side, and all about himself, and in, really, a style so vain and so silly as to surprise and almost disgust me. I suppose something that I happened to say may have made him guess that I was *somebody*, and he went out of the room for a moment, I have no doubt to ask the office-keeper who I was, for when he came back he was altogether a different man, both in manner and matter .... In fact, he talked like an officer and a statesman.... Luckily I saw enough to be satisfied that he was really a very superior man; but certainly a more complete and sudden metamorphosis I never saw.'*

The superiority came out in talk on the military situation, the balance of power and the fighting chances. It was the old story: genius for one function, and folly in the normal situations of life.

But a far more damaging record is the history of Nelson's conduct towards the republicans of Naples, as now placed beyond doubt by Italian investigations.† Flattered to fever-point—never a difficult thing in his case—by the King and Queen of Sicily, he committed on their behalf, but of his own zealous choice, an act of infamous treachery. Finding that, just before his arrival at Naples, the republican garrisons had surrendered on a treaty of indemnity with

* Croker's *Correspondence and Diaries*, 1884, ii. 233; Captain Mahan's *Life of Nelson*, ii. 322.

† See the *English Historical Review*, April, 1898; and compare Captain Mahan's *Life of Nelson*, i. 430-444, where Nelson is first defended—without knowledge of the later published Italian documents—and afterwards partly blamed.

The Militarist Regimen

the King's Vicar-General, Ruffo, and the commander of the English squadron, he first proposed to break the treaty; and then, when the Italian honourably and inflexibly refused, he resorted to an act of fraud unparalleled in modern military history. In the words of Mr. F. P. Badham,

' He made a feint of falling in with Ruffo's ideas, and in carefully-studied words, intended to deceive, he promised that he "would not oppose" the execution of the capitulation. Once the garrisons were embarked Nelson laid hold of the vessels, and made the republicans prisoners. In fine, Nelson started with the premise that it did not matter what one did with Jacobins, and with this all his subsequent proceedings were in accordance. Under circumstances of peculiar illegality and unfairness he kidnapped and hanged the republican Admiral. He waited for more than a week, making scarcely any effort, while Naples was exposed to the unspeakable horrors of a sack by the convicts and bandits whom Ruffo had recruited in Calabria. He delivered over more than 8,000 prisoners to the royal vengeance. He uttered no word of intercession while a Royalist Reign of Terror, every whit as merciless as that of Arras and Bordeaux, was established in Naples. And in all this, as Captain Mahan has pointed out, his conduct was dictated by no sort of English interest: he completely subordinated his position as English representative to his allegiance to Sicily.'

It has been asked whether or not Nelson was incited to this infamy by Lady Hamilton, who, furious as he against all republicans, and as crazily devoted as he to the Sicilian crown, had her mission from the Queen: 'Recommend Lord Nelson to treat Naples as if it were a rebel town in Ireland. Finally, a severity exact, prompt, just: the same for the women, and that without pity.' But Adam was as ready for evil as his Eve. The man whose whole rule of life for his midshipmen—a rule transcended, one hopes, by most of the men who to-day sweep our streets—was, 'Fear God, honour the King, and hate a Frenchman as you do the devil,' needed little prompting to any act of savagery towards Jacobins. As Mr. Badham puts it,

'There was an anti-revolutionary fury, we must remember, as well as a revolutionary—white Jacobinism as well as red. Only a few months before the period under discussion the murder of the French Ambassadors at Rastadt had been condoned by monarchical Europe with a mere shrug of the shoulders. And of this anti-revolutionary fury Nelson had a peculiarly sharp attack. Republicans of every shade are for him "infamous Jacobins, felons, infidels, robbers and murderers," but "their measure of iniquity is nearly full, and God is in the act of chastising them." To another correspondent: "Your news of the hanging of the thirteen Jacobins gave us great pleasure, and the three priests will, I hope, soon dangle on the tree best adapted to their weight of sins," the sentiment in this case being the more remarkable from his knowing that at Procida, where these thirteen had been condemned, prisoners were not usually allowed to be present during trial. Again: "Our friend T. had a present made him the other day of the head of a Jacobin, and makes an excuse, the weather being hot,

The Militarist Regimen

for not sending it here." On another occasion he even stoops to : " Exact as degrading terms as it is in your power to give. No covered waggons, no protection for rebels !" '

Such a man was England's supreme Admiral. And because this energumen had the genius of naval strategy, and twice signally defeated the naval enemy of the moment, we are still called upon by our energumens of empire to cherish his memory and hallow his name. To such a code can patriotism bring us. And it is with such examples before them that our accomplished advocates of militarism can claim for military life the merit of preparing men for the civil. Probably few will dispute that the naval exploits of Nelson might have been performed by Paul Jones, had he been a British Admiral. He had certainly the genius of naval strategy, and a boundless courage. Well, the biographers sum up that with it all he was a man of inordinate vanity and detestable moral character. With a much less faulty character, it is not pleasant to think what part Nelson as peer would have played in those English domestic troubles which so swifty followed on English victories. Enough for his career, in the eye of a sane posterity, will be the acted evil thereof.

IV

To some on first challenge all this may seem to be mere special pleading, if not something worse. When we reflect what multitudes of men have unquestionably remained honourable and chivalrous gentlemen after a longer or shorter military or naval life, there may well seem to be something of perversity in an argument which dwells mainly on the seamy side of the careers of great commanders and military States. And it is possible, of course, to make out the case against militarism onesidedly. Some onesidedness there is, perhaps, in the remarkable work of M. Hamon on *Le Militaire Professionel*, which, some years before the outbreak of the Dreyfus scandal, arraigned the army as a school of lawlessness. It is not difficult to pick from military biography stories enough of fraud and rapine, baseness and egoism, to make out a black case.

As everyday life, however, presents the same features, to the knowledge of every man of the world, there is a risk of fallacy in reasoning from the symptoms to the special environment. One might make out a similar case against University professors, men of science, scholars, artists; an American inquirer has actually

The Militarist Regimen

undertaken to prove, by a laborious research, that the clergy in the United States furnish a larger percentage of crime of all kinds than any other of the learned professions—nay, than the general population. It might plausibly be argued, on the other hand, that certain types tend to gravitate to certain professions; but here again we are faced by the fact that there are honourable men in all. The real issue, therefore, is that above examined—the value of a military training as a preparation for civic life, or for any other than purely military functions. It is perfectly fair, then, to form an opinion on the historic evidence as to the fate of fighting peoples and the statesmanship of great captains. Ensign Newcome leaves the army Colonel Newcome, a more admirable gentleman than he was when he entered it; but the process of mellowing would have gone on quite as well outside. Regimental life does not make saints out of sinners, or gentle spirits out of egoists. Rather the question rises whether even the Colonel Newcomes do not miss a needed intellectual discipline; and when we come to the rank and file, there is hardly any question at all. Complaisant publicists tell us in private how useful is the army as a training-school for coachmen and valets; how it takes slouching and turbulent types and makes them shaven, upright, orderly, biddable, and respectable. It may be so: there is no institution which does not yield some relative good; and it would be unfeeling to refuse to rejoice with the plutocrat in his possession of a steady coachman. But we are considering the total influence of the trade of arms, and meeting apologists who say it is good for all, not merely for a recalcitrant residuum; and we are further arguing from the point of view that the dominance of the militarist ideal is one of the main hindrances to a social science which would provide other ways of humanizing the defective types.

Now, for every larrikin that the army licks into vertical shape it turns two potentially average minds, capable of development, into superior forms of domestic animal, without intellectual initiative, and without the desire to have it. A model veteran is as often as not a model child in intelligence; and the veterans who are not models hardly help the militarist case. But we may put a more general test, asking of the institution as a whole, whether a habitual practice of blind obedience is conceivably productive of good judgment in anything. The necessarily negative answer points to the most charitable view that can well be taken of the conduct of the French military authorities in the Dreyfus case.

The Militarist Regimen

Reading one revelation after another of shameful fraud on the part of some, and incredible shallowness of judgment on the part of others, we begin to ask whether the French staff is mainly composed of knaves and fools. The answer is, first, that in an army the knaves, be they few or many, are far more potent than elsewhere, just because of the nature of the system; and secondly, that they accordingly have less difficulty than elsewhere in making fools of the honest men, who there are made less competent than elsewhere to detect knavery. No lay jury could commit such a travesty of justice as was accomplished by the court-martial on Dreyfus; and no lay institution would dare to resort to such a campaign of subterfuge and suppression to cover an error as was undertaken by the French staff.

Such an episode is a specific fruit of militarism. Only national conceit can lead Englishmen and Germans to believe that a similar case is impossible in *their* armies; indeed, some Germans readily avow that analogous cases are privately known to have occurred in Germany, where it would be impossible to have them reopened. Bismarck would have scoffed at the thought of letting a court-martial's injustice be exposed; and it is to be remembered that one of the first intimations made by English correspondents of the movement to reopen the Dreyfus case was accompanied by an emphatic opinion that it was better to let even an innocent man suffer than to set up an army scandal. It is the irreducible aversion of uncorrupted men to such a doctrine that has made possible the climaxing protest in France and elsewhere. And in this connection it is worth while to note how the moral courage needed to begin it was found only among civilians. To Emile Zola go all the foremost honours of the fight. No soldier dared face the suborned multitude as did he; not till the defence had waxed powerful in prestige as well as in moral force did an officer come forward to aid it. It is not on the battle-field or the drill-ground that men learn, if it be ever learned, the lonely courage that faces domestic hatred and the hiss of the crowd; and where such courage is needed in the strifes of civil life, it will assuredly be none the scarcer for the stopping of the school of the slayer.

If, however, it be urged that military men are not fairly to be suspected of lack of moral courage because their sense of discipline keeps them out of a movement which impeaches their superiors, we may rest content on the position that they are proved to be weakened

The Militarist Regimen 109

by their training for the exercise of judgment in matters equally open to the verdict of laymen and to theirs. This is the upshot of the recent discussion among ourselves as to the fitness of Lord Kitchener's conduct in desecrating the tomb of the Mahdi at Khartoum. It is made clear by the very arguments of the defence that the act—one of military politics—was a lapse from common-sense as well as from decency. One set of apologists tells us that the fanatics had to be disabused of their notion that the Mahdi had ascended bodily to heaven; another set tell us that if the body had been left in the tomb, the same fanatics would be sure to make pilgrimages thither, and pilgrimages might lead to revolts. As if Christians had not made nine crusades to recover and keep the tomb of *their* prophet in the full belief that there was no body there, and in the full knowledge that it had been desecrated for ages by two races of unbelievers! The surest way to undermine the Mahdi's prestige would plainly have been to show that the conquerors had no fear of it, and attached no more importance to his tomb than to any other. By rifling his tomb and insulting his corpse, they have done their best to renew the fanaticism which they had half discredited by simply defeating it. We are finally told that the act had been advised by Mohammedan officers. It was what the Turks would have done in such a case. Need more be said?

V

We shall be called back, perhaps, to the contention that there is civic value in a military training which stops short of actual war—a moral value that outgoes the mere physical gain to a volunteer from camping out. It is somewhat odd that this plea should be urged precisely among the peoples who have no conscript system, no universal militarism; and one is moved to ask whether Captain Mahan, for instance, really supposes the youth of France, Germany, Russia, Italy, and Turkey, to be at once more law-abiding, more thoughtful in politics, and more fit for industry and commerce, than the youth of the United States and England. Such appears to be the implication, and it is a surprising one. Those of us who have discussed the point with educated but non-official Frenchmen and Germans who have done their due drills, are not often met by any such opinion. In France, it may be confidently asserted, there grows, step for step with the advance in the efficiency of education, a conviction that the years spent in military training are a wretched waste of time; and the commonest feeling among the better-educated men during their term of service is one of contempt towards the officers who voluntarily embrace such a profession. Some small countervailing benefit there may be in the contact of the less-educated men with their superiors, but I do not find that good and close observers attach much weight to such an influence from their own experience. They do not find the backward types amenable to it; and on the face of the case it is clear that such influence must at best be a poor makeshift for a culture that ought to have been undergone in boyhood. You give a boy a bad schooling, take him away half taught, set him to hard work in his growing years, and then claim to give him a physical and moral boon by drilling him for certain terms in the company of other youths, of whom a few are more fortunate. As a deliberately chosen scheme, it seems hardly less than farcical. If we are to plan at all for social betterment, we had need plan some worthier method than this.

Turning to the special case of Germany, where, barring perhaps Turkey, militarism is at its maximum for scope and thoroughness, let us put another test. Germany is still, on the whole, the most highly educated nation, and in the past its writers have had a great influence on the moral judgment of the rest of Europe. Kant, Schiller, Herder, Goethe, the Humboldts, Herbart, Richter, Fichte, Fröbel, Schleiermacher, Raumer, Feuerbach, Gervinus, Vogt, Bluntschli, Marx, Lassalle, Wagner, Freiligrath, Heine—all these, to name no others, had in their various ways a specifically *moral* influence in Europe, over and above their vogue on other grounds. But while German specialism still ranks at least as high as any in most departments of pure research, who now recognises any moral impact from the later German literature ? We are concerned to know what Germans think on most points of learning and science, but who greatly cares what view a German of the majority takes on any question of right or wrong ? Who, save a militarist, respects any German ideals save those of Socialism, which are the negation of militarism and Bismarckism ? It is the bare truth that German ethical opinion has no longer the slightest prestige, and the reason is the double one that the ruling German ideal has lost all virtue to the deeper moral sense of men, and that the leading German writers of these days make no impression of moral inspiration. To a thinking reader, unswayed by a foregone theory, Mommsen is seen to have become the

The Militarist Regimen 113

mere immoral mouthpiece of the Bismarckian ideal, a partisan degraded by race prejudice below the level of worthy historiography—in short, a false historian, however erudite. Scholarship is one thing, and moral weight another. There is positively not one well-known German historian since Burckhardt and Döllinger whose opinion on any moral issue need give us pause. From Russia come the moral ideas of Tchernichevsky, Dostoievsky, Tolstoy; from Scandinavia, those of Ibsen and Björnson; from France, those of Guyau, Zola, and, till the other day, Renan; but from Germany, apart from academic systems which miss the general mind, what? The one recent German writer whose moral ideas have arrested European attention is Nietzsche, the *revolté*, the most un-German of Germans; and he is impressive precisely because, whether in the really high ethic of his earlier work, as the *Zarathustra*, or in the wildly wandering doctrine of the years of his decadence, he stands for something freer, purer, and sincerer than the official gospel of German imperialism.

Now, this state of things is unintelligible save as a product of the system of Bismarck, the reign of Moltke, the modern millennium of the drill-sergeant. Either the acceptance of that regimen has paralyzed the German spirit on the moral side, or the better German minds dare not speak out. That they dare not is asserted by those who ought to know; ethical teachers are said to find themselves morally gagged. But that implies a moral prostration of the general mind around them; and such a prostration can result only from the stringent operation of forces that were absent or only half-grown in the Germany of half a century ago—rabid militarism, nationalism, monarchism, imperialism, Chauvinism, servile bureaucracy. A dramatic episode of a few years ago brought out in a flash the depth of the transformation. In some restaurant, an officer collided somehow with a civilian, and, feeling himself affronted, drew his sword. The civilian ran away, but the officer pursued, overtook him, and ran him through. So went the reports, which further stated that the Kaiser, on being consulted, held the officer blameless, and expressed a hope that his officers would always thus prove themselves the guardians of their own honour. Right or wrong, the story is let pass without question by typical military men. I once spoke of it, in another country, to an experienced Prussian officer, and received the emphatic and serious answer, 'Ah, that was honour!' For him, the question was so settled; it was a matter of honour for an armed man to

The Militarist Regimen

slay an unarmed, who fled from him. One can but say that such honour stands rooted in dishonour, and that the ethical ideals of a nation where this one passes current can count for nothing with free men anywhere.

Only a long reign of militarism, the eternal adversary of right feeling, could bring such a people to such a pass. In a future age, unless haply we are all already in full decadence, it will be reckoned a sufficient measure of the worsening power of militarist imperialism that within the first ten years of the present Kaiser's reign the prosecutions for *lèse-majesté* were counted by thousands, and included many lads in their teens. The evils of commercialism are indeed many and deep; but in so far as they are proximately natural, as results of an ingrained system that to most of the sufferers seems unchangeable, they do not demoralize and paralyze as do the evils of a tyranny imposed from without, resting on naked force and the mere habit of submission, and removable by an act of national will if the will were there. There are few displays of self-satisfaction more fatuous than those of the German professors who to-day felicitate themselves and their pupils on an imagined superiority of virtue and viability in the Teutonic over the 'Latin' races. They who suppose that mere study, mere thoroughness of specialism, can make valid men out of subjects who dare not so much as jest in each other's hearing at the foibles of their Emperor, are already on the way to Byzantine conditions. Better fifty years of factious Paris than a cycle of Philippine Madrid; thrice better when Paris alone breeds the Velasquez.

If philosophizing militarists, German or other, were given to viewing comprehensively the relevant facts, they would be struck by the circumstance that the European country which to-day shows least of progressive virtue is relatively the most militarized. Turkey, glared upon by envious Christian eyes at every point of her horizon, misgoverned, fanatical, impoverished, ignorant, yet maintains an army that, relatively to her resources, is immense in numbers, and obstinately efficient for its purpose. The one continuous national effort made by Turkey is military, unless we reckon as national the almost universal support given to Islam. Where other States spend more or less freely on public schools, Universities, technical education, the arts, and sanitation, as well as armaments, Turkish public expenditure is practically concentrated on military schools, barracks, warships, and war material, with or without proportional pay to troops. It would puzzle our militarists to detect the resulting civilization in the lives of Kurds and Bashi-Bazouks, or in any habits of skilled industry; though there seems to be plenty of respect for a constituted authority that deserves none. The apologists would seem here to be driven to the argument that for Turkey militarism is a necessary evil. If, indeed, any Government in Europe can justly offer the plea, it is the Turkish. But here, at last, we come to the truth that militarism *is* an evil; and if only *that* could be brought home to the general consciousness of Europe, the plea of necessity would not long avail.

VI

With the case of Turkey under our eyes, and the successive sophisms of militarism at length wheeled out of the ring, we come to close quarters on the counter-theory—that war is an evil of evils, and that the perpetual preparation for it cannot yield a balance of good. One leaves the direct impeachment to the last, because it is meat and drink to the militarist to be met by that while he is full of his undissected sophisms, conscious of anti-sentimentalism, and confident that it is mere sentimentalism that is opposed to him. It has by this time become fairly clear that he is himself the typical sentimentalist, the true visionary, the amateur in logic, and the tyro in sociology. And it is now for him to see to the defence of his last ditch.

That war is somehow a test and evocation of true manhood is the ethical assumption that underlies all of the apologies. As held by Mr. Ruskin and others who have acclaimed war without understanding it, the doctrine rests upon the notion that war is essentially a trial of strength, of endurance, of fortitude. That it is this in some measure, like racing and leaping, is true; but that it is so first and last is the delusion of men who have never studied it, or the sophism of men who have. There never was a time when war did not tend to turn upon special cunning or special advantage, rather than upon the fair trial of strengths. In the warfare of savages, the differentiation is towards ambuscade and nocturnal surprise — devices which when successful, our militarist will infallibly tell us, amount to superiority, and convict the vanquished of inferiority, in vigilance, which is a form of strength. Thus does the unfair, the furtive, the merely cunning, begin to figure as a military virtue from the start of the ethical discussion.

When the furtive virtues are developed all

The Militarist Regimen

round, however, through the survival of the furtive fittest, advantage must be sought in other ways; and, after some development of drill and discipline, a new species of weapon is the likeliest new departure. The combatant with the better weapon develops his moral manhood by that means, and the less inventive is wiped out as being less manly. As time goes on, successful manhood tends to consist, belike, in improving the weapons of defence, and the better man is he with the better breastplate, before which the heart untainted will fare ill. If Shakespeare ever penned the imbecility, 'Thrice is he armed that hath his quarrel just' (and the verse-tests are all against the attribution) 'why, then, the less Shakespeare he.' Here, happily, the militarist and we of the opposition are at one. The Greek victory over the Persians at Plataea seems to have been due in part to superior discipline, but mainly to the wearing of defensive armour, a safeguard which the Greeks in their own previous wars had forced on each other. Every step in the development of war is primarily an effort of one combatant to get the better of the other by an unforeseen trick; and the question is whether such an evolution is decently to be described as a testing and evocation of true manhood.

Patriotism and Empire

At certain stages, the normal tussle may for a time come very near being an unskilfully honest trial of strength. Before the Battle of Leuctra, the Greeks seem to have gone out to fight each other without any anxious regard to superiority in numbers, and with pretty nearly equal weapons. They drew up in opposite lines, came together, and straightforwardly hewed at each other in a way that we can agree with the modern militarist in regarding as unintelligent. Save insofar as the Spartans practised a constant and strenuous discipline, they were all merely testing their manhood in the fashion of bulls and stags, not to say cats and dogs. But at the Battle of Leuctra, Epaminondas had an inspiration. He saw that by dividing one half of his line in blocks and moving them diagonally towards the remoter end of the enemy's line, while the other half of his marched on it in a straight advance, he struck that half of the enemy a twofold blow,* and could so destroy it; whereafter, with only the slight loss he had incurred in fighting one half of the enemy with two to one, he could

* Mr. Grote oddly supposed that Epaminondas won by keeping his centre and right 'comparatively out of action,' while his left, in deep formation, fought the Spartan right. The whole point of the plan was that the Theban centre and right should follow up the blow of the left.

The Militarist Regimen

attack the other half with nearly the same advantage.

In its origin, the manœuvre was rather moral than scientific. The part of the Spartan line at which Epaminondas first struck was made up of the Spartan troops proper; he knew that if he annihilated them their allies would make no great fight. Were it not for this racial or moral motive, reinforced by the fear that the dreaded Spartan hoplites might overthrow an equal body of his own troops, he might never have dreamt of such a stratagem; and only the slackness of the allies, with perhaps the use of his cavalry in checking them, left him free to overwhelm the Spartan right.

Such was, broadly speaking, the fortuitous beginning of scientific tactics. Epaminondas' device was adapted by a hundred later commanders, as by Frederick at Leuthen, and by Napoleon, with perhaps greater subtlety, at Ligny. The sentimental militarist is committed to calling these strategic successes evocations of manhood; the unsentimental civilian is moved, on the other hand, to regard them as at best victories of fox over wolf, of adroitness over mere courage. We might as well see a test of manhood in the strife of an unadvised layman with an unscrupulous attorney. Critical admiration we may give to the finesse and ingenuity of the victor, but the less said about ethical implications the better.

In simple fact, then, we find that the so-called Cobdenite ideal is almost chivalrous in comparison with the ideal of calculated war. The word 'chivalry' comes to us from a time when knight was supposed to meet knight with no thought save of a fair trial of strength, with haply some intervention of deity. But we have only to note the evolution of the knight's armour to see how preoccupied he was with the betterment of his chances. Nay; outside of the knightly class he never had a grain of scruple in riding down the unarmoured footman. The business of the medieval general was to neutralize the knight's advantage, whether by archery, by the ring of spears, or by pits and calthrops. The English boy is taught to glow at the thought of the advantage his ancestors had over the French in their use of the bow; the Scotch boy learns to rejoice in the foresight with which Bruce at Bannockburn kept five hundred horse ready to hurl on the English archers, and dug pits and laid spikes in them for the English knighthood. Thus is our manhood attuned to higher issues.

The question for the cold-blooded civilian is, How can the sentimental man of war get any pleasure in the thought of the trick or ad-

The Militarist Regimen

vantage which enabled him to win the battle? Pride in one's speed or strength is intelligible, though not admirable; but pride in having won a race by tripping a competitor—pride which in a genuine trial of strength would demonstrate baseness—how does it become manly in anything that pretends to be a trial of strength? The pretence is an imposture. '*All* is fair,' so runs the adage, 'in love and war'—in the battle, that is, of men, and also in the battle of the sexes, as regarded by the men who approve of the other. The moral advantage would appear still to lie with commerce. The story of a manufacturer who ruins a hundred poorer producers by temporarily underselling them is still unpleasant to the ear of the smoking-room; it is only when the principle is applied to warfare, and the dangerously courageous inferior races are mowed down with machine-guns, that we thrill with entire satisfaction.

Perhaps the best way to undermine sentimentalism about war would just be a general course of instruction in naval and field tactics; for though the man of war must needs sentimentalize in order to sustain his self-respect, the instructed civilian is apt to lose taste for the thing. The mere explanation of tactics is singularly disenchanting. In that modestly entertaining work, *The Life of Captain R. W. Eastwick*, there is a plain and unvarnished account of how, in the year 1799, the English frigate *La Sibylle*, commanded by Captain Edward Cook, son of the circumnavigator, captured the French frigate *La Forte*. The English ship carried forty-four guns, and was very fully manned; the French carried fifty guns, but was greatly undermanned, having sent off many drafts of her crew with prizes. Coming up by night, the English ship covered her guns and lights, and, not firing when fired upon, contrived to make the Frenchmen believe she was an Indiaman. Not till within two cables' length did the *Sibylle* suddenly unmask her lights and open fire. The crew of *La Forte* did their best; but their vessel being abnormally high in build, her guns could not be so laid as to come to bear on her assailant at such close quarters, while the lower ship sent every broadside easily to its mark. For an hour and forty minutes the unequal fight lasted, till on the *La Forte* out of three hundred there were fifty-five killed, including the Admiral, the Captain, and the first, second, and third Lieutenants, with eighty-five wounded, while on the English vessel there were only fifteen killed and wounded, the enemy's fire having mostly gone over the heads of the crew. Then the last French officer, a boy, struck his colours; and good Captain Eastwick, who has honestly noted all the facts, tells how he, a prisoner on the French ship, exulted in the cheer of the victors. 'It filled the welkin with a glorious sound which recorded the accomplishment of a great deed, and I felt my heart beat faster, and my blood go rushing through my veins with pride.'

Such are in sooth the greatest deeds of war —successes in beating an opponent whose hands are virtually tied behind his back. The English Captain was fatally wounded; and when he died soon after at Calcutta, the East India Company gave him a monument in Westminster Abbey, whereon it can still be read that, 'after a long and *well-contested* engagement,' he had captured a French frigate of 'very superior force.' Knowing how one such glorious victory has been attained, the civilian mind grows somewhat hardened concerning others. The Battle of the Nile, for another instance, was made known to many of us in our school-books as a 'brave story' that 'can never die of age.' But the school-books did not enlarge much on tactics; and perhaps, if they had, we should not at that age have been disillusioned by the explanation. What happened, as we learn in later life, was that Nelson, finding the French fleet anchored fairly close inshore, wrought a stroke of strategic genius by sending some of his ships between the enemy's line and the shore, and the rest on the outside; thus putting eight of his to five of the enemy, and in some cases three to one, the others being unprepared to move; and so destroying first one half and then the other. It was brilliant strategy, one more variant of the move of Epaminondas; but to exult in it when one knows how it was done, and to look on the result as a noble evocation of manhood, is not easy to the unsentimental landsman. There remains, of course, the sentimental landsman, who the other day figured in his old character in the United States, bestowing on an Admiral who beat a wooden fleet with an ironclad fleet as high praise as ever was given to any of his predecessors. Still, other landsmen were found to wince.

The principle of being always two to one is manifestly prudent, nay, scientific, but not romantic. And that is the gist of war, according to Napoleon, one of its mightiest masters. The business, as he summarized it, consists in so marching on your enemy that you outnumber him at the point of battle, and do him the maximum possible injury. We can but say, inverting the Frenchman's comment on the charge of the Light Brigade, *Ce n'est pas mag-*

nifique ; et c'est la guerre. That which is morally magnificent is not war, and that which is war is not magnificent.

VII

'Not magnificent' is indeed a mild way of describing war as we now begin to know it—those of us, that is, who have either seen it or can realize it when competently described, or, perhaps one should say, who are willing to know what that is that they tacitly or actively conserve. M. Verestchagin has recently told us how 'a very well-known Prussian general advised the Emperor Alexander II. to have all my military paintings burned as objects of a most pernicious kind.' That general was well advised, from a professional point of view. A wide circulation of truthful pictures of battle-fields would make it painfully hard to keep up the conventional enthusiasm about fighting; and if the after-battle photographs taken in the American Civil War had been generally familiar to the people of the States, there would have been less promptitude about the attack on Spain. In the scarcity or absence of pictures, however, there begin to accumulate a certain number of word-pictures, and it is well to have some of these in view when we form our opinions about the moral value of militarism. The sentimentalists, of course, would have it otherwise : for them war is ennobled by being abstracted ; but we must respectfully insist upon their having the courage of their opinions.

A notion of the real significance of war begins to be brought home to the civilized world by the works of some of the artists who have done most to make fiction deserve the praise of being the highest truth. It is, indeed, denied of M. Zola that his truth is sufficiently representative ; but I doubt whether those who thus impugn his realism will apply their objection to his great epic, *La Débâcle*. However that may be, and however Tolstoy's pictures of war may be held to be discounted by his gospel of non-resistance, it will not be denied by many outside of the school of Mr. Henley that Thackeray is the truest painter of life and character in English fiction ; and it is from him, the creator of Colonel Newcome, that there comes the demand: 'Why does the stately muse of history, that delights in recording the valour of heroes and the grandeur of conquest, leave out these scenes, so brutal, mean, and degrading, that yet form by far the greatest part of the drama of war ?'—the 'burning farms, wasted fields, shrieking women, slaughtered sons and fathers, and drunken soldiery cursing

The Militarist Regimen

and carousing in the midst of tears, terror, and murder.' It is from him, too, that we get this vignette of Esmond's experience in one of the campaigns of Marlborough, in a raid on Artois and Picardy:

> 'The wretched towns of the defenceless provinces, whose young men had been drafted away into the French armies, which year after year the insatiable war devoured, were left at our mercy; and our orders were to show them none. We found places garrisoned by invalids and children and women; poor as they were, and as the costs of this miserable war had made them, our commission was to rob these almost starving wretches—to tear the food out of their granaries and strip them of their rags. 'Twas an expedition of rapine and murder we were sent on: our soldiers did deeds such as an honest man must blush to remember. We brought back money and provisions in quantity to the Duke's camp; there had been no one to resist us; and yet who dares to tell with what murder and violence, with what brutal cruelty, outrage, insult, that ignoble booty had been ravished from the innocent and miserable victims of the war?'

Thackeray and Zola are likely to be long read; but the unsentimental sociologist may do well to recall to his antagonists a more ephemeral utterance, that, namely, in which the *Times* correspondent briefly pictured the Battle of Sedan:

> 'Let your readers fancy masses of coloured rags glued together with blood and brains, and pinned into strange shapes by fragments of bones. Let them conceive men's

bodies without heads, legs without bodies, heaps of human entrails attached to red and blue cloth, and disembowelled corpses in uniform, bodies lying about in all attitudes, and skulls shattered, faces blown off, hips smashed, bones, flesh, and gay clothing all pounded together as if brayed in a mortar, extending for miles, not very thick in any one place, but recurring perpetually for weary hours; and then they cannot, with the most vivid imagination, come up to the sickening reality of that butchery.'

That the production of such effects as these, the battering of so many myriads of human beings into immeasurable dung, should rank as a splendid activity, a test and evocation of the highest manhood, is surely a remarkable proof of the power of sentimentalism and claptrap in human affairs. That the scientific control of the business stands for a considerable mental activity is, indeed, not to be disputed; and it is intelligible that men should find the science of the matter interesting, though it seems odd that any should find it pleasant. But if it be again pretended that this form of mental exercise counts for anything in solving any other sort of human problem than those on which it is primarily exercised, one must plainly say that the claim is a piece of quackery. The mere combination of military genius with superior intellectual powers of any other kind is rather the exception than the rule. Even the sane and accomplished Cæsar has not left us a memorable thought, any more than a plan for human guidance; and Alexander could never have made a name in any path of peace. The normal concomitant of military capacity is simple steadiness of judgment and action, never depth of insight into any social or other non-military problem. Napoleon's ideas on economics were childish to the last. Frederick, most philosophic of Kings, was but a vigorous repeater of the ideas of his teachers. Washington was a man of commonplace understanding, unique only in his tenacity of purpose. Cromwell was an ordinary fanatic in everything but administrative faculty; as a constructive politician he was naught. Marlborough, one of the supreme captains of modern history, was in peace a dullard, and was almost devoid of the moral sense. Wellington and Nelson, so different in temperament, were alike in being Philistines of the Philistines. Lee and Grant, exceptionally likeable men both, would in all likelihood never have been heard of but for the Civil War. Moltke is a modern superstition. He never fought against a great general or a really well-appointed army; and that his ideals should be held up to our respect is the measure of the intellectual indigence of those who share them.

Let the experts make as much as they will

of their science ; but let them know that as to the moral side of their vocation a good many of their contemporaries emphatically endorse the words of one who has seen war and handled its abominations, and who does not deal in word-painting:

'I can understand that men find a pleasure in studying the art of fighting, as they do in playing a game of chess; and I have allowed in my own case the fascination which even its horrid reality is capable of exercising over me. But for the man who deems it a pleasure and a glory to use the science of war as a weapon wherewith to annihilate thousands of human beings, for the delusion called 'prestige' or in the game of politics, I would have him to know that it is a foul and monstrous thing, full of hideous suffering, cruelty and injustice, with nothing to redeem it save the courage whereby such miseries are endured.'*

VIII

In fine, if the militarist ideal and the practice of war are to subsist in the future as in the past, mankind will have something like a sufficient proof that the belief in moral progress is a hallucination; that what happens is only a change in the rhythm of evil. Military persistence in the habit of thanking God for every successful massacre of what are alleged to be

* Dr. C. E. Ryan, *With an Ambulance during the Franco-German War*, 1896, p. 254.

The Militarist Regimen 133

God's creatures begins to bring the evil more directly home to the modern intelligence, instead of glozing it as of old. Ethics apart, it is too revolting to mere common-sense. The reign of the old ideal is strictly the reign of stupidity; and the resort to the old practice is stupidity in action, whatever intelligence be brought to bear on the *ultima ratio*. To realize the sheer intellectual incoherence of the minds that make for war, it suffices to read one sequent and careful study of the politico-military history of one nation in one generation, the *Down with your Arms* of the Baroness von Suttner. One of the leading articles in the creed of our sentimentalists is the unfitness of women for political life. But a woman has been too much for the militarist party, so far as logic goes, in one of the leading military States. Her work is the demonstration of their political incompetence, their intellectual shallowness, their puerile instability of thought and purpose.

That the politics of peace, of anti-militarism, are intricate and obscure is only too true: that is one of the conditions of the prosperity of militarism. It is perfectly true that merely to abolish or greatly reduce armies, were that speedily possible, would create a new economic problem, or worsen an old one, in place of the moral problem grappled with. In so far as

134 Patriotism and Empire

there are sentimentalists of peace who do not realize that a genuine social science is not a simpler but a harder thing than the science of war, the cause of peace is ill bestead. If the social righteousness of the rational does not transcend the social righteousness of the sentimentalists of slaughter, there is no hope for social sanity. Rather, the friends of peace and reason must base their campaign against war on a scheme of social science, seeing in militarism not only a substantive evil, but a profound vitiation of the industrial problem. Instead of taking that up with an eye to a permanent provision for labour and a maximization of real wealth, we are being led by our patriots into a more and more precarious inflation of industry by way of an increasing expenditure that creates no wealth whatever, and in reality adds to the mass of parasitic life. Certainly the problems of society hang together. But that is no reason for keeping on a course which essentially aggravates all of them.

It is not proposed here, when the comparing of counsels on the subject has but begun, to offer a detailed scheme of action towards the gradual withdrawal of armaments, the substitution of a rational machinery for the settlement of national differences, and the simultaneous provision for a sound in place of an unsound

The Militarist Regimen 135

development of industry. But the commonsense lines of a method of proportional disarmament are not hard to sketch. Assuming the scheme of arbitration agreed on at the Hague Conference to be a sufficient beginning on that line, the friends of peace have next to agree on a balance of naval power as between the six or seven leading naval Powers, the balance to be struck not as they at present stand, when some are overtaking the special efforts of the others, but in terms of an average of their relative strength during, say, thirty years, or any other considerable term which may be agreed on. A given relative strength being settled, every nation could without misgiving limit itself to merely replacing, in terms of agreed - on standards of fighting force, the ships chronically lost in the edifying manœuvres of peace; or, it might be, the decay or loss of certain ships might be made a basis for a proportional dismantling of vessels by other Powers. With average good faith, and with freedom of mutual inspection allowed to all the Powers concerned, the scheme could be worked well enough, if only there were the will.

Then, given the operation of such a scheme of naval restriction, the same principles might just as easily be applied to the restriction of armies, making, say, the year 1875 the date from which to calculate the relative strength of the chief European Powers. It is known that Bismarck many years ago was ready to consider a scheme of proportional disarmament; and though he had by the annexation of Alsace-Lorraine put the worst of all possible obstacles in the way of such an adjustment, as between Germany and France, it is not impossible that the growing spirit of Socialism among the workers of both nations may evolve a compromise in the coming century. If not, it will not be the élite of the workers who are responsible, but the exploiting class which everywhere sees in militarism the surest check to democratic aspirations, and which to that end fans continuously all the embers of old hate among the peoples.

To abolish war, then, there must first be a war of ideas. Yet if the saner spirits throughout the world would but strive for a generation to promote peace with a tithe of the energy that in nearly every State has been incessantly spent on war and its works since the dawn of history, the issue would not be doubtful. Certainly it is a tremendous 'if.' The other year we saw the civilized United States, after a relatively trifling effort to promote peace and quietness in Cuba, zealously spend enormous sums and immeasurable effort to add systematic destruc-

The Militarist Regimen

tion to the long record of Cuban evil. Thus are civilized men still constituted; and their political ethic must change ere their fortunes do. Let the peacemakers look to it. Their work is not to evoke for peace any such burst of blind emotion as is so easily evoked for war, but to build up mankind in a spirit of reason —a task for a lifetime.

PART III
The Theory and Practice of Imperialism

I

IT is when we come to the outstanding political problem of the period—the problem signalized by the word Imperialism—that all our issues come into their clearest light. Patriotism, conventionally defined as love of country, now turns out rather obviously to stand for love of more country; and the militarism urged upon us as a fountain of domestic virtues comes out once for all, in our own case, as a needed instrument of foreign expansion. The three ideals are solidary. But a special set of pleadings emerges on the new issue; and in relation to it the others take on special phases.

No change in the drift of British politics since 1870, perhaps, is more marked than that set up in the prevailing tone of allusion to the colonies and dependencies of the State. It is

Imperialism

since Mr. Gladstone's death, however, that the tide has flowed highest. In the years of Disraeli's ascendancy, from 1874 to 1880, the 'imperial idea' had indeed been swiftly and successfully grown, to the point even of overshadowing Gladstonian Liberalism. On a policy of naked aggression, ungilded by any clear appeal to commercial interests, the adroit leader of the Right was able to detach vote after vote in the House from his rival's side; and we know that he at length believed he had thrust Gladstone out of power for twenty years. The crushing overthrow he met with in 1880 was the decisive measure of the relative strength of the two men as creators of opinion. What Disraeli had done was to exploit the normal temper of Chauvinism on such opportunities as then came in his way; and as a party policy, morals apart, his course was quite astutely chosen. There was no better way to play off elemental force against elemental force; and only the thorough adequacy of Gladstone to the contest, with his gift of evoking and even creating equally strong and simple instinct on a higher plane, made possible so severe a check to so prosperous a movement. The two men spontaneously adjusted themselves to each other's strength and weakness—a thing not seen in our politics since, and perhaps not again to be seen; since the days of one-man-leadership would appear to be almost over.

A powerful national tendency that has not discredited itself, however, is not to be destroyed in politics by merely pitting against it in one election a contrary tendency: the check is only temporary, and the struggle is but postponed, with a probability meanwhile of gain in strength to the checked movement. The state of political culture which had made possible the accession to the Disraelian policy of a score of Liberal votes in the House, and of several journals in the Metropolis, was not changed. Gladstone was an inspirer and commander rather than an educator; he had really no constructive ideal fitted to oust the other, and he was hardly settled in office when he found himself carried into strictly Disraelian courses. Of each and all of them he duly repented; but his lapse was the expression at once of his practical empiricism and of the real strength of the forces he had seemed to conquer. They consisted, roughly speaking, of (1) the 'service' interests, which since his own abolition of purchase in 1871 had become knit as never before with the middle class; (2) the specifically capitalist interests, which were directly involved in Egypt, and were already reaching out towards South Africa; (3) the general trading interests, which spontaneously leant to 'expansion' as a way of widening the market; (4) the temper of national pride developed in the latter-day commercial aristocracy and rich middle class, as of old in the aristocracies of feudalism, and of the landlord system of last century. The forcing forward of the Home Rule issue by the skill and strength of Parnell in 1885-86, and the energy with which Gladstone fought it up till 1893, kept that issue in the forefront, and called off to it the forces of imperialism, which were now nearly all arrayed on the side of Unionism, and were thus organized on a new tactical basis. But when the defeat of Home Rule was followed by the withdrawal and death of Gladstone, and his lieutenants, for lack of a common ideal, decided to keep no constructive policy whatever before the nation, imperialism inevitably began to carry all before it.

A nation, roughly speaking, must be ruled either by moral ideals or by appetite; by the critical spirit or by the acquisitive spirit, by its reformers or by its self-seekers. Often, indeed, the latter types hold each other in balance, and so arrive at compromises; but if one side is for the time torpid, the other is sure to be doubly active. Many of the reforms of the last seventy years have represented the coincidence, in a measure, of appetite and moral ideal, as in the combination of employers and workers to overthrow the Corn Laws; many others represented the coincidence of moral ideals with party interests, as in Disraeli's Household Franchise Bill and Gladstone's act of Irish Disestablishment.

In other instances, decisions taken on grounds of party tactic came to be held on the tenure of the moral ideal which best justified them. But if neither party interest nor class interest supplies a platform on which a moral ideal can stand, and no party will determine to build up its interest round such an ideal, it is hard to see how the reign of appetite is to be curtailed. The interests which have no rag of higher morality to cover them need but put on the draperies of immemorial instinct, national egoism, and pseudo-philosophy, in order to sit in the chair of rule. Such a dominion is now in process of creation; and just as in the days of Palmerston and Disraeli professed Liberals were found leaning to the doctrines of swagger and conquest, so at present, when Liberal leaders disclaim them, professed organs of Liberalism announce that 'we' do not share the abstract objection to expansion. Imperialism, in short, is the prevailing fashion of political thought. And as its enthronement infallibly means an increasing plague of militarism, and a fresh florescence of the spurious ethic of patriotism on the lowest planes, it behoves us to consider narrowly its pedigree and its pretensions.

II

Some dispute has arisen in England over the claim of some professed Liberals, that there is a 'true' as against a 'false' imperialism, and that what they affect is the true. Comprehensively speaking, the asserted difference is that between the view that 'empire' as thus far evolved is a very fine thing, and the view that a very fine thing ought to be still further developed. Obviously, those who take up the latter position have an advantage. England has been 'expanding' during a century and a half, and it is implied by the party of 'true' imperialism that the expansion has been a profitable and laudable process; why then, on that view, should it not continue? Why not aim at a British China as well as a British India? It seems to be supposed that if the empire-building of the past be pronounced aught but beneficial, the critic is committed to advising the immediate evacuation of India, a course which, as will be elaborately and gravely explained to him, would plunge India in anarchy. Of that very obvious proposition, however, we may make a common ground for a somewhat more extended theory of imperial policy.

That India must for an indefinite time continue to be administered by the British State is a truth in no way affected by any opinion we may form (1) of the process of its acquisition, (2) of the effect of its possession on British civilization, or (3) of the effect of British or any other rule in perpetuity on Indian civilization. If, then, the 'true' or 'sane' imperialism consist broadly in the determination to go on ruling India as far as possible for its own good, we may, as true or sane imperialists, discuss all three questions; and by such inquiry we may conceivably reach a justification for the refusal to attempt, say, duplicating our Asiatic empire in China. Many of our politicians instinctively feel that the policy of extension is blind and ultimately fatal, but beyond quoting Augustus and Trajan they attempt no sociological analysis, and, as aforesaid, they feel committed to speaking of the existing empire as a thing wholly glorious. They have thus no principle or ideal to set against the ideal which the expansionists claim to sanction by that very attitude; and in practical politics their principle of staying as we are is well-nigh hopeless. To argue that we have already secured just the

Imperialism

right amount of beneficent empire, no more and no less, is nugatory as against men who say we cannot have too much of a good thing. The 'sane' imperialist, then, if he would hinder further expansion, must make out a case against that ideal of imperialism which primes expansionism ; and if he does this, he will find that he must condemn the theory of imperialism in the lump, while recognising the exigencies of the situation it has thus far created. Empire is one thing, and imperial*ism* another. The latter term may with special fitness stand for the ideal which not merely accepts made empire and makes the best of it, but holds the pursuit of empire to be either at all times, or specially at the present time, a course scientifically advisable in the interests of free and rationally governed nations. It is in this fit and natural sense of the term that it is here henceforth discussed.

III

And first as to the pedigree of the principle and the practice. The average citizen who talks of empire is not very clearly conscious that he uses a word which properly means 'rule'—rule over other communities than his own. As applied in the phrase 'our colonial empire,' it is already diverted to a merely geographical sense, seeing that the colonies neither pay tribute to, nor receive laws from, the mother-country. Even the Sovereign is 'Empress' only of India, though the convenience of the expression 'the British Empire' has fixed it in use for the whole connections and possessions of the United Kingdom. But it is the more important to remember the historical meaning of empire, seeing that it is at empire, in a slight modification of the historical sense, that imperialism aims.

The significant thing is that, to say nothing of the most ancient known military empires, which grew out of the conquest of city by city, the most expressly 'free' or democratic of the communities of historic Greece coveted empire from the instant it became possible to her. It was the determination of Athens to coerce her allies, already made subservient to her gain by the spending of their quota on her public works, that provoked the Peloponnesian War, which brought her empire to an end. And that her policy of imperialism was politically fatal remains clear whether or not we argue that any other course was then conceivable for her statesmen. Either Athens must dominate all Greece by becoming a purely military power like Rome, in which case her democracy and her culture must go by the board, or she must be ruinously beaten back to her separate status. It was indeed to the loss of her empire that she owed the fresh growth of her culture in the generation after the war, whereas Sparta, having evolved none but militarist institutions, was as bare of intellectual life after the fall of *her* empire as she had been before. But the principle of empire once admitted, in the lack of the wisdom that could see its universal fatality, there was in store for Hellas nothing but one convulsive and coercive military unification after another, down to the advent of the Roman. After the rule of Athens, the rule of Sparta; after that, again, a limited Athenian rule, got by triumph over the Olynthian confederacy; then the Macedonian rule, based on the military experience of Thebes; then, on Alexander's death, the new swarm of Hellenistic empires; then the advent of the Roman, doomed to the same dissolution. In every instance the progression is one of social disintegration under the guise of military advance: decay of public spirit in Athens; decay of the Spartan ideal in Sparta itself; decay of vigour in the post-Alexandrian empires; decay of class cohesion in Rome; decay of the whole Roman system under the autocracy.

148 Patriotism and Empire

Not that there would have been no social problem but for imperialism; on the contrary, the Periclean system is seen to stave off the social problem at Athens for the time being; but the process is merely one of evading the Sphinx riddle till the Sphinx's claws have clutched. From first to last imperialism conforms to that formula. Instead of solving the social problem by science, each community in turn strives to set up unity for its clashing classes of parasite and drudge by making them collectively parasitic upon other communities. The plan, of course, is not clear. The initial motives are instinctively military, and in the case of Macedon the social problem has not yet clearly arisen; but for all alike the question in time becomes one of sheer self-maintenance by conquest and domination. Athenian empire began with the 'glorious' repulse of the Persians; and in this ancient triumph the degenerate Greeks went on glorying long after the Romans had put them under the yoke. But the curse of militarism ensues all the same, whether its installation come by way of defence or of aggression. The triumph of the Syracusans over the tyrannizing Athenians was followed by the tyranny of their own Dionysii; the pride of Marathon and Salamis was the prologue to the fall of the Peiræan walls; and

Imperialism 149

had there been no Persian War, the Athenian Empire and its ruin need never have been. The social problem might or might not have been solved, but at least it could hardly have failed to be faced by later Solons.

As it was, democracy was distracted in the direct ratio of the military stress. The social problem bears a slow solution; military problems do not. Always the choice is being forced between some honest incompetent Nicias and some capable dishonest Alcibiades: the non-democratic enemy has always the possible advantage in singleness of policy, and though the democracy tends to produce the larger crop of capacity, the democratic method can least well utilize it. Thus in the second empire of Athens 'we see her sending out general after general to recover some ancient possession or to put down some new enemy, and in almost every case accusing the general, on his return, of inefficiency, negligence, or treachery, and visiting these offences either with a severe fine or more commonly with death.' Thus arises the opportunity of Philip or of Alexander, of the skilful plotter or of the great captain. Democracy must fall; and though the first sequel of its fall be a free play of its remaining energy in the intellectual life, the blight of autocracy ere long destroys that, and we have left only the mindless and soulless peace of pretorian-guarded Rome.

Subjectively considered, the course is no less clear. It begins in the spirit of injustice; the lust for rule over others on the part of the man who claims freedom for himself; the demand for tribute by the man who hated to pay tribute. Common honesty as between city and city would have excluded the possibility of empire; but seeing that even the measure of honesty that subsisted between citizen and citizen was but a conventional marking out of the lines on which one citizen should be free to live idly by another's labour, it was above the moral range of the group to discern the dishonesty of seeking to draw a common revenue from the resources of another community. A Socrates in the earlier day of Pericles could have pointed out that the policy of extortion as against other cities could only make enemies to the plundering city; and if the Socratic method had then elicited the truth that such extortion was only an application to intercivic policy of the private practice of the men who constituted the cities, the Socratic inference would only have been the clearer all round. That inference the Greeks could not draw. It remains to be seen whether it can be drawn by the nations of the twentieth century of the Christian era.

IV

One of the most unpromising symptoms of our case is the uncomprehending way in which the British imperialist always scans the story of ancient Rome. Noting the decadence which is the upshot of the whole, he seems to suppose that somehow Christianity will avail to save later empires from the same fate, though Rome was Christianized during the decline; or that haply the elimination of chattel slavery will avert decay, though Christian Spain was free from chattel slavery at home; or that industrialism will avail, though the Moors and the Florentines were tolerably industrial. Any theory will serve to burke the truth that the special cause of decay is just empire.

Yet, as regards Rome, the sequence is as obvious as any in human affairs. In the post-regal period the spirit of patriotism enabled the ruling class to turn the whole fighting power of the community to the oppression of neighbouring States; and the social problem, always being raised by the utter egoism of the exploiting upper class, was chronically staved off, essentially at the expense of the subjugated neighbours, by way of the planting of Roman colonies on their soil, and formally by granting one political privilege after another to the plebeians. The patrician reluctance to make such concessions was extreme. Twelve years after the first Secession of the Plebs, Spurius Cassius (B.C. 486) paid with his life for proposing, as Consul, to distribute some public land among needy citizens, and to draw State rents from the rest. The nobles saw in the public land their proper patrimony. Thirteen years later a tribune was murdered; and seventeen more years elapsed before the Icilian law could be passed distributing some land at Rome to poor citizens. Political strife between plebs and patriciate continued to alternate with the wars in which they were united; and a new line of cleavage and adjustment began in the paying of the soldiers, while the nearer neighbours, the Latins, had to be admitted to some Roman privileges. Still, the social evil remained uncured; and after many Roman and Latin colonies had temporarily relieved the strain, there were passed by plebeian pressure (B.C. 367) the Licinian laws, relieving debtors of interest, limiting estates, and calling on landlords to employ a certain proportion of free labour. Such laws could not be enforced; but now, in virtue of fresh conquest, the unprivileged Roman class could so force its claims on the aristocracy that they were by degrees sub-

Imperialism 153

stantially blended in a community of exploitation of other States. A new populace infallibly grew up in place of the old; but henceforth the stuff of the populace, bred under the code of national plunder, yielded no material capable of valid initiative.

The consolidated Romans could now wage an imperialistic war with the rival Samnites, who had preceded them as overrunners of Southern Italy, and the nearer Latins, who pushed their claims to Roman privileges; and after generations of war, breeding a whole caste of trained captains and administrators, all Italy became Roman (B.C. 266) on various conditions of subjection. Thus imperialized, the conquering State rapidly proceeded to foreign war and new conquest, the ancient Roman farmer class all the while dying out; the popular element in the government disappearing in favour of the Senate; foreign tribute coming in to enrich the latter; and gladiatorial games arising to amuse the imperialized populace. Twenty-three years of war with Carthage might be said to fix the Roman destiny of conquest; and diplomacy, as well as the Illyrian War, introduced the Senate into the affairs of the Greeks.

Thus far, needless to say, it was a matter of course that Rome should be militarist, were it only as against the barbarians of the North; so that there could be no question of pause on the part of the administrative class. Between barbarians, Carthaginians, and the Kings of the Alexandrian succession, it was a struggle for conquest on all hands. Our business is not to censure the Roman Senate for a policy of which no man could then impeach the general wisdom, but to note how, in an age of struggle for empire, the successful State was demoralized in the ratio of its success; and then to ask whether a modern State does sanely to aim at empire when no such destiny is in any sense forced upon it. Within a generation of the subdual of Italy, a Roman literature, imitative of the Greek, had begun. In two centuries of aristo-cratico-republican imperialism, as in a hotbed of artificial stimulus and protection, that literature had reached its high-water mark; and thenceforth, under autocratic imperialism, it decayed as rapidly as it rose, till, the brains being out, the empire in the West fell before a rabble of barbarians. Men fix their gaze on the roll of early conquests, the final triumph over Carthage, the acquisition of Spain and Sicily, the defeats of Macedon and of Antiochus, the controlling of the East, the acquisition of Greece; but they will not see that every gain was a step nearer the break-up of the Republic. To say nothing of the incessant influx of alien

Imperialism 155

slaves, ousting the native stock, every fresh evasion of the ever-renewed social problem meant a further step towards the state of quarrel among the ruling class themselves; every acquiescence of the common people in a solution by way of outside plunder lowered them nearer the status of a pleading proletariat. The imperial people was *ipso facto* a community diseased; and wherever they imposed their rule they infected with decay the subject States.

Let it be asked how the decay could anywhere have been arrested without modification of the ideal of empire, and the fatality will exhibit itself at any point of approach. The senators, it is clear, ought to have aimed at preserving a free farmer class, instead of seeking for large estates tilled by slaves. But the senators were seekers of plunder and dominion abroad, and how should they love fraternity and freedom at home? They should have preserved agriculture, as a way of checking the depopulation of Italy. But they had conquered better grain-lands than Italy; and when they could extort grain as tribute, or grow it cheaply in Sicily by slave labour and sell it in Rome at a profit, how should they concern themselves about home agriculture and population? They were personally comfortable enough. It would have been well to renounce the importation of hordes of alien slaves, who loved Rome little and could not be trusted to fight for her. But then, slave labour served their luxurious wants; and their patriotism meant readiness to fight and conquer and plunder in Rome's name, not self-denial to keep Rome sound. The less cynical complained of the decay of public spirit. But when had public spirit meant anything but seeking one's own interest through the State's? It was only a question of new methods of self-seeking. Legal restraints passed into disregard; how should conquerors, educated in coercion of the conquered, retain the habit of abiding by law?

Thus, within a century and a generation of the subdual of Italy—a century which saw the mighty effort of Hannibal and its end—the imperial Republic had but arrived at being a scene of aristocratic wealth and plebeian poverty on a larger scale, with outside Italy clamorous, impoverished, unfriendly, and with no faculty left to cure the evil. The two Gracchi in their tragic way exhibited the futility of the method of force, the inability of the military spirit, even when beneficently bent, to apply any other. The first based himself on the selfish Roman populace, who would not make common cause with the Italian peoples; the second, with larger views and capacity, based himself on the claim of the Italians to equality; both alike had against them the main mass of the selfish and furious nobility; and both duly paid the penalty. But Caius ere he died had called out a new force of cleavage by making the middle-class *equites*, the money-lenders and tax-farmers, a counterpoise to the Senate. As posterity put it, he 'made the Republic double-headed.' He would have overthrown the whole system; and with his constructive energies he might have built up a new and mightier empire, whose downfall might have been longer delayed. As it was, his brother and he had only pointed the way to the rule of the sword in civil dissension. Henceforth the throes of the convulsion come fast: after Marius, as servant-master of the troubled State, comes the bloodier Sulla; and had not Cæsar overthrown all, Pompeius had, with no very different sequel. For persistent empire in the end infallibly brings the imperator, be the process slow or speedy; and with the imperator comes in due time the decadence of empire, the humiliation and paralysis of the spirit that had aspired to humiliate its kind.

V

Not once in a thousand years does the lesson seem to have dawned on any people. After all the imperialisms of the Middle Ages, we find the citizens of free Florence, as late as Savonarola, no less bent on empire than those of Periclean Athens. Because they had once held in subjection the neighbouring city of Pisa, they would rule Pisa to the end, at whatever cost of blood and enmity, denying her the independence they claimed for themselves. Machiavelli and Savonaralo are two opposed extremes of type: the one a subtle rationalist, the other a Puritan fanatic; but both alike stood by the dogma of dominion over Pisa. We might say that a Florence with such an ethic did not deserve to remain free; but it may be more to the purpose to note that she could not. Her little empire was the millstone round her neck in the struggle for survival.

Nearer our own life, we find the England of the fourteenth and fifteenth centuries all for empire over France. The men who at home had chronically to struggle for their own liberties were at all times ready to be united in

Imperialism 159

a project for subverting other people's; and no experience of the infallible sequence of evil could cast out the spirit which dictated the aggression, though as time went on it became less feasible. Not in medieval history is to be found a more perfect illustration of the curse of empire than the sequel to the conquest of France by Henry V. The steps are the old series, quickened and complicated: first, evasion of home problems by patriotic attack on a neighbour; second, triumph; third, division and decadence on the scene of conquest; fourth, gross demoralization, humiliating defeat, infamy, expulsion, end of empire; fifth, civil war at home, with utter demoralization, lasting until the military class is exhausted; sixth, the advent of a new dynasty of imperators. During a century of empire, defeat, effort towards new empire, and loss thereof, feudal England produced not one lasting name in literature; nay, it took another hundred years of comparative peace to raise letters to the height at which Chaucer had left them.

In that interval there had arisen the first modern empire which rivalled in range and power that of ancient Rome. Spain, bred to arms by the long struggle with the Moors, added province to province, heritage to heritage, conquest to conquest, till her King held in thrall Peru and Mexico, Italy and the Netherlands,

> 'Tunis and Oran, and the Philippines,
> And all the fair spice-islands of the East.'

And never did the sheer possession of empire more signally entail decadence, paralysis, ruin. Much was due, assuredly, to the monstrous cancer of the Inquisition; but then it was the ideal of empire, rooted from the first in the feud with Islam, that at length made possible the special supremacy of the Inquisition in Spain. Religious tyranny stayed its feet on the necks of conquered Mexico and Peru; and among the better Spanish brains struck down by the Church when they would advance on her doctrine, there can have been few who had not exulted in their country's conquest and dominion over the heathen beyond seas. Empire, once more, had made the imperator; and imperator and priest, going hand-in-hand, alike drawing the gold supplied by the conquered lands, could strangle every effort at new thought and new faith.

Englishmen, in the eternal way of national vanity, set it down to their stock that they developed differently. But had England possessed the same empire, and been able so to live on extorted bullion, the same sequence

Imperialism

could perfectly well have arisen in her case. It was the possession of foreign mines of gold and silver, and other forms of unearned wealth, that atrophied the industry as well as the intelligence of Spain; the intellectual disease furthering the other, above all when the Church's insanity availed to expel the Moriscoes. Not a nation in Europe but would have clutched joyously at the same deadly possession. But the England which could beat off the great Spanish Empire at the very acme of its power was the 'Little England' of Elizabeth, the England of Shakespeare and Spenser and Bacon, so trivial a territory now in the eyes of the patriots of the England of Mr. Kipling!

Had England been able, again, to play the part played in Europe by France under Louis XIV., there was in her the spirit to do it. Cromwell at his death had launched on a policy of reckless imperialism, attacking Spain by choice as being weaker and more easy to plunder than France; and had he lived, forced as he was to seek revenue by conquest, he might have gone far. But dynastic interests and strifes kept England out of the field while France, passing rapidly from a standing army of eighty thousand to one of four hundred thousand, reaped victory, glory, empire, decadence, and exhaustion, till the Little England of Anne could humiliate her, as Elizabeth's had humiliated Spain. The strife of dynasties and parties in England prevented the pressing of her advantage ; but her day of empire was to come. It began, broadly speaking, under the first Pitt ; and, with waxings and wanings of the spirit of militarism and conquest, it has subsisted till our day, and will subsist yet a while. Because her fortune thus far is better and her state healthier than those reached by Spain in the seventeenth century and France in the eighteenth, her sons assume that for her there is no fatality in empire, no law of decay. Let us then narrowly scan her special problem.

VI

The one circumstance which greatly differences England's empire from those of Rome and Spain is her advance in industry step for step with her advance in empire. This immensely important difference is plainly due, not to any quality of race or special wisdom of policy, but, after the political antecedents, to the natural conditions on which her industries specially rest. These are abundance of coal and iron. Before empire could become a source of national income, at a time when normal commerce had set up commercial and

Imperialism 163

industrial ideals, and when the other leading European States had their energies otherwise occupied, first a series of mechanical inventions, and soon after the application of steam to machinery in general, set her people upon using their coal and iron to an extent that began a new industrial era. Her empire was thus from the first rather subservient to her industry than subversive of it. Where Rome and Spain became entirely parasitic, she continued to be productive; and though latterly her land has begun to pass out of cultivation like that of imperial Rome, and her imports greatly to exceed her exports, like those of imperial Spain, the order of causation is so essentially different that thus far her power is not impaired. But a clear order of causation there is, and the study of it reveals the probable sequel.

Cromwell's policy having been arrested, English empire broadly begins with the dominance of Chatham, and in his hands the policy of empire was the natural sequence to the older policy of combination against France. Walpole, for dynastic reasons a convinced believer in peace, held by his alliance with France, and opposed a war with Spain even after those two thrones had made a private compact to undermine England's commercial power. It was the Spanish policy of trade monopoly that at length forced war, at the instance of the commercial classes, on the unwilling Walpole in 1739. Habitual English smuggling, in breach of the Spanish monopoly of Spanish-American trade, was naturally met by the Spaniards with measures of search and punishment; and resentment of these was the immediate motive of a war by which, of course, the trading class hoped either to capture the monopoly or break it down. Needless to say, the English were as much bent on monopoly for themselves, wherever possible, as the Spaniards; and when in 1725 the Austrian Emperor, as titular head of the Holy Roman Empire, gave a trade charter to an Ostend East India Company, the English and Dutch Governments had alike protested. For the rest, Spain had in 1718 striven to abet the Stuart Pretender, and national conscience was nowhere scrupulous about making war. Walpole and his French contemporary, Cardinal Fleury, had been almost the only European statesmen of their age who really sought peace and ensued it. In Spain, after the Peace of Utrecht, Cardinal Alberoni had the wisdom and the fortune to break down the internal restraints on trade, and the immunity of the nobles and clergy from taxation; but in

Imperialism

him the ideal of empire dominated all others, and he had turned all the gain to fresh aggression.

The war which began in 1739, and which, by embroiling England with France, led to their later struggle for empire in Canada and India, might have sufficed to discredit the policy which made it. After nine years of strife, in which England, as ally of Austria, fought the futile battles of Dettingen and Fontenoy, and the no less futile naval battle of Toulon, everything returned to the *status quo ante bellum*, with the question of trade absolutely hung up. The Powers had merely exhausted each other; and in 1755, having recruited, they resumed their grapple. On the side of England, in the strenuous hands of Pitt, the new war was at once much less commercial in motive, and more propitious to the lower commercialism in practice. He is the best of the modern imperialists, a proud seeker of national honour rather than gain, and an inspirer of the same temper in his countrymen. Collective gain-seeking, in fact, was as yet a lust without collective intelligence. The Spanish War had been, as we have seen, a noisy futility; and Law's Mississippi Bubble in France, and the South Sea Bubble in England, had demonstrated only the immensity and imbecility of the appetite for unearned gain, a thing Pitt never sought for himself, and was not concerned to help others to seek. There was probably more of systematic commercial purpose in the counsels of France, whose empire fell in Canada and India not more through want of coherent administration than through the insupportableness of the strain of a first-rate land war against Frederick in Europe, along with that of a first-rate naval war against England. Pitt's policy of enormous subsidies to Frederick was not that of a seeker of money gain. It is the more important to note that imperialism in this, its most grandiose form, does but in the end subserve nevertheless the dominion of wealth and the spirit of self-seeking.

Walpole had reduced the National Debt in 1739 to forty-seven millions; in 1748, at the Peace, it stood at seventy-seven millions; in 1763, after the Seven Years' War, it had reached one hundred and thirty-nine millions. The vital meaning was that to the extent of the interest on that sum a parasitic class was now definitely added to English life; and no idealism on Pitt's part could hinder the sequence of evil. Systematic Parliamentary bribery, involving the buying and selling of seats outside, had been begun by Walpole; Newcastle continued it at

Pitt's side; and after Pitt's fall the method was carried further than ever under the hand of the King. System for system, that of England had already grown as corrupt as that of later republican Rome; and the saving force was in no sense empire—for the class now enriched from India was at least as corrupt and corrupting as any—but the increase in industry which proceeded in virtue of the natural conditions. While the upper classes scrambled shamelessly for unearned spoils, real wealth was still forthcoming at the hands of those grimy heathen colliers and pallid factory hands among whom Wesley and Whitefield went evangelizing.

What could come of mere empire was first seen in the loss of the American colonies, as soon as imperialist finance was applied to them. So far had imperialism gone that (apart from the few typified by Chatham, who thought first and last of keeping the empire united to make head against France, and the few typified by Burke, who further looked to the question of trade) Englishmen in general certainly approved of coercing the colonists. And but that their hands were full in Europe, where they were fighting France, Spain, and Holland, and in India, where they were fighting Hyder Ali, the King and his Ministers might have carried their point in America for the time being, leaving the reaping of the whirlwind there for the next generation. With the National Debt increasing by annual leaps, with war on their hands in three continents, they still had the support of many for the new declaration of war against Holland in 1780, because in the City 'the spirit of gaming had seized all ranks, and nothing was thought of but privateering.' It was in the worst spirit of plunder that the Dutch War was waged, and it was well for England that the triumph of the colonies altered her course.

The severance was precipitated by the King's stupidity; but it was only a question of time. Seen as a humiliation by all her rivals, it was for England in reality a wholesome rebuff; and though the upper-class hatred and fear of democracy could soon afterwards plunge England in war with republican France, her imperialism had been for the time checked at its roots in popular feeling. Practically, it was still a Little England that finally baffled Napoleon, as formerly Louis XIV. and Philip II. The wealth accruing from India was as nothing for purposes of warfare: it was only by means of monstrous additions to her already immense debt that the younger Pitt was able to play his father's game; and those additions were made possible only by the still more rapidly increasing industry of

Imperialism 169

the nation. And it was the renewed industry of France which, after the termination of *her* Napoleonic empire, brought to her a renewal of wealth and culture and civilization. Not plunder and violence, but labour and peaceful commerce, were the creative forces for both nations, loaded as they were with the debts of their wars of mutual frustration.

VII

After Waterloo, it seems to have been realized by the intelligence of Europe that militarism and imperialism had alike pierced the hands that leant on them. As against the former chronic death-grapple for some arbitrary 'balance of power,' even Conservatives held by non-intervention; and the loss of the colonies to England, no less than the decadence of Spain, had shown the vanity of foreign possessions. In England, the old arrogance for a time bade fair to cut off Canada; but the new spirit was strong enough to avert extremities, and a relatively ethical if sociologically empirical belief in the virtue of industry as the right ground of a nation's greatness took for the time the place of the dream of prestige and the passion of racial enmity. With Cobden figuring as a national and even as an international force, a sane ideal of civilization seemed at least to be shaping itself. Macaulay, writing on Clive in 1840, professed astonishment at the apathy of his generation to the story of the rise of British empire in India. An Anglo-Indian Liberal, writing just after the Indian Mutiny, sharply retorted that the reason was plain enough, though Macaulay would not confess it. Englishmen, he said, were ashamed of the story—a comment possible only at a time when imperialism was in low repute. After the Crimean War it probably went still lower, in Macaulay's despite, with the credit of militarism in general; for no war had ever been more flagrantly convicted of stupidity alike in the deciding and the waging. Among thinking people, the one countervailing thought was that wrought up by Tennyson in his *Maud*—the ignobleness of so much of the life of peace as carried on by those who decried war.

And herein lay, not, certainly, a rational defence of militarism, but a clue to the fundamental evil which made militarism still possible: the ancient schism of rich and poor, which had broken out afresh in England ere the Waterloo bonfires were cold, and which in France had at last made the way for the Second Empire. Industry and its abstract ideal, the honest rendering of service for service, had so far

Imperialism 171

withstood all the social maladies set up by the evil ideals of the near past; but it brought its own, or, rather, it did but alter the incidence of the oldest social malady of all. Under industry as under feudalism, barbarism, Greek democracy and Roman aristocracy, the ultimate success, the practical ideal, is still the power to live luxuriously without rendering any service. Speaking not deductively and ethically, but inductively and historically, we may safely say that the definite preponderance of that ideal in any State is the beginning of the end. The preponderance of the reverse ideal would *a fortiori* be the beginning of a new life, but from such preponderance every State is yet far. In France, the moneyed class could overthrow the mid-century republic, after the republic had overthrown the moneyed class's monarchy; and significantly enough the new empire revived militarism to the uttermost of its power, though it intelligently enough encouraged industrialism at the same time, by way of pacifying its proletariate. Striving to check discontent by more imperialism, it went down as every empire one day must; but in the Third Republic as in the others the social problem presses hard and steadily. Hence, though that problem is visibly much aggravated by militarism, there arises a source of motive power for militarism over and

172   Patriotism and Empire

above the still unslain spirit of racial enmity. In England, with differences of time in the hot fit and cold fit, the same contagions work to similar effect; and in Germany the discord between the ideal of empire and that of Socialism is full of evil promise.

It behoves us, however, to analyze in particular our own problem. Here, latterly, the strife of classes has been on the whole less marked than in Germany and France, the movement of imperialism having rather forestalled than followed industrial pressure. Pressure there has been; but the relative elasticity of English trade conditions, turning as they largely do on the readily alterable rate of coal-supply, has thus far averted a crisis. The crisis, however, lies ahead; and in the imperialist movement is to be seen a half-instinctive reckoning on it. It is seemingly felt on all hands that, between competition and the expanding power of machinery, our trade is within sight of its limits; that the existing field of investment is all laid out, and that in some creation of 'new markets' his to be found te only cure that the case admits of. A leading statesman has put the idea in the memorable proposition that we must 'open up new markets in the waste places of the earth.' In that egregious saying lies implicit all the commercial theory of the situation. The primary object is not to buy, but to sell, and receive goods in return to sell again; all to the end of heaping up more capital for investment. Our own toilers are not to do more consuming, to begin with: it is not their lot that is in question; at most it is assumed that they can prosper only through the prosperity of capital.

How far a distinct conception of this kind is a primary stimulus to imperialism we need not inquire. Without doubt, the mere pride and passion of nation and race are still the prime factors with many, as in the case of the Disraelian imperialism of 1876-80. But the concept of commercial interest does emerge more and more distinctly, and it is to it, finally, that appeal has to be made to carry the point against criticism. We have specially to consider, then, the elements of the commercial argument, taken with and without the notable profession of disinterested zeal for the welfare of the human race, or at least of the lower races, which commonly embroiders it.

VIII

Shortly put, the imperialist's case is that expansion of 'the empire' is necessary—

(1) To provide openings for the emigration of our superfluous population; and

(2) To 'open up fresh markets.'

When answered that we need not own our markets, and that trade normally goes on between different States, he answers,

(3) That 'trade follows the flag.'

Incidentally he is apt to point to the benefits bestowed by British rule on the natives of India and Egypt; and he is at times led by the exigencies of argument to affirm that the bestowal of such benefits is his and his nation's master passion; though the previous propositions might be supposed to invalidate it for the intelligence even of the lowest races concerned. It is fit, however, that the pleas should be weighed singly as well as in collocation.

And first as to the formula about scope for emigration. Only actual observation could convince one that this plea is ever used in good faith, so nakedly does it collide with the notorious statistical facts. A glance at the Registrar-General's returns shows us that year by year from two to six times as many British emigrants pass to the United States as to all the colonies together. Between 1853 and 1897 there emigrated from these islands nearly eight and a half millions of British and Irish-born subjects; and of these, over five and a half millions went to the States, against little more than two millions who went to British colonies. The emigration figures for 1895 stand:

> United States . . . 195,632
> Australasia 10,809
> British North America 22,357

six going to the republic for one that went to the colonies.

Furthermore, the regions in which alone there is any ostensible prospect of 'expansion' in the near future are precisely those which offer least outlet for genuine emigration: to wit, China, uncolonized Africa, and parts of South America. Those, then, who first put forward the 'outlet' plea were either ignorant doctrinaires who did not seek the most elementary information on the issue on which they offered counsel, or persons who had not the excuse of ignorance. It belongs to normal human nature, however, that worthless arguments, once floated, should be caught at by people conscious of having no other, and therefore glad to believe in any put in their way; and one sees this impudent absurdity gravely vended in reputable Liberal journals, and by citizens incapable of framing the frauds they endorse. Thus does imperialism make headway.

But supposing that the desired expansion

were really a means of relief to surplus population, the theory on which such relief was sought would be only the clearer an illustration of the hand-to-mouth ideal involved. It is implied that there is to be no social science, no control of population by reason and knowledge, no provision for it at home by better use of the land; nothing but a fatal drift of blind instinct and blind competition so long as emigration can take place, and after that the deluge. And as other nations, in the terms of the theory, must be mostly in the same case, our ideal is to let the deluge fall on them. The Germans, with an increasing and largely poor population, partly profess the same belief in colonies as outlets; the French, with a stationary and therefore a less poor population, seek colonies where they do not colonize, and hardly pretend to do so. The struggle for life, then, lies between such States as Germany and England; and all other European peoples—Spaniards, Italians, Swiss, Dutch, Scandinavians—are on the new population theory doomed to speedy misery, Russia escaping for the time in virtue of her vast territory. Meantime England and Germany must fight to the death; and the surviving nation will go on till, even the States being full, the human race goes to ruin for want of the sense to restrain its rate of breeding.

Imperialism 177

Such is, in its logical development, the social *Welt-Anschauung* that rules the hour.

To turn from the theory to the facts is to realize once for all the character of imperialist sociology. It is a tissue of false conclusions from falser premisses. Germans, like Britons, are found emigrating wholesale to the United States. Of 224,000 German emigrants between 1893 and 1897, 195,000 went thither; and so long as emigration is the accepted solution of the problem, it is there open to them as to anybody else. Italians emigrate alike to North and South America, settling in myriads under alien flags, while their misgoverned motherland spends blood and treasure in a senseless clutch at waste places about Abyssinia. Swiss, Dutch, and Scandinavians either limit their families or emigrate to the all-receiving United States. The claim, in short, that this one country must for its own preservation from distress head off all others in confiscating territory from the lower races, is a rather weak variation on the classic plea of the Wolf *versus* the Lamb.

Putting aside, then, the 'pasteboard portico' of the pseudo-Malthusian theory, we come to the real motives: (1) The primary desire of the speculative commercial class for new grounds in which to buy cheap and sell dear; (2) the suffusive instinct of spoliation and dominion which, on the part of the services and the general public, backs them up; and (3) the sinister interest of those industrial sections which thrive on the production of war material. It would be hard to conceive a more mindless system of social evolution than that presupposed by the resort, at this time of day, to the early ideal that trade is best to be pushed by barter with semi-barbarians. In the seventeenth and eighteenth centuries, as temporarily in ancient times, the pursuit and proffer of exotic products enlarged commerce and consumption and the arts of life. In our own day we have found that, with an ever-increasing production of export and import goods, there is no proportionate heightening of consumption and of the arts of life among the mass of the people. The true problem, then, is not to induce more uncivilized people to buy our products and pay for them with theirs, but to increase the consuming power of the producing masses already interchanging. A raising of the standard of comfort among our own mass, a substitution of decent conditions for hideous misery among the lower strata of the imperial State, would at once widen markets in an indefinitely progressive degree; while no amount of expansion in Asia and Africa, as things now go, can conceivably lessen our own normal rate of

Imperialism 179

pauperism. Nay, the imperialist implicitly claims that such expansion will alone avert an increase in our imperial pauperism. How perfectly insane, then, or how grossly sectarian, by his own showing, is the ideal he would have us embrace! Imperial England has proportionally more and worse poverty than almost empireless France; much more than Switzerland, Holland, and Scandinavia. Such are the fruits of imperialism; and the prescription is, More imperialism!

It will at this stage be argued, perhaps, that English industrialism, centring as it does on the process of exhausting the coal-supply, is incurably artificial as compared with that of most other countries; that we must 'dree our weird'; and that the way to do so is just to keep up the pace till, with the end of superiority in coal, the game is up, and our empire and civilization crumble together. That some such notion is behind some of our imperialism is likely enough; it would in fact be the soundest possible statement of the imperialist case in terms of imperialist practice and economics, though the majority would probably be loath to avow as much. But supposing the case to be put with such hardy cynicism, or, let us say, pessimism, the answer is again plain. If English civilization is in a way to fall to decadence as soon as the coal is gone—and on the present lines it must infallibly so fall—it is the business of sane Englishmen, not to quicken the pace and hasten the ruin, but to substitute sound bases for the unsound as carefully, yet as quickly, as may be.

As matters stand, the experts promise us some fifty years more of fairly abundant coal and iron, and then a closing of most of our blast furnaces. The crisis may come even sooner; for if the immense mineral resources of the United States are developed with modern rapidity, that competition alone might suffice to ruin the English trade before coal has actually become scarce. Meantime, the very policy of expansion itself may destroy the home industry it is professedly undertaken to further. Already the cheap labour of India and Japan is made the basis for a new competition with British manufactures; and our politicians are found staying themselves on the unspeakable theory that the radical cure would be bi-metallism, since that would put our currency on all fours with the Eastern. Let the 'break-up of China' only go on as our European plotters would wish, or let China merely develop in Japanese fashion, and the unmeasured coal and iron deposits of the Chinese territory, with the enormous mass of cheap Chinese labour,

Imperialism

may rapidly be brought into the competitive field. In that case British capital will go whither it can find most profitable employment; and as population, under the present social system, must needs pass away when industrial demand falls off, the empire of England will be a tale that has been told. All of these developments are perfectly likely on the face of the case, yet not a word of them do we hear from the patriots and politicians who hound on the people to further empire. Not a finger, all the while, do they move to give England once again that root in agriculture which should save her from becoming a deserted dust-heap while France and Spain haply grow richer and happier in virtue of their enduring relation to the forces of production. And not a hint, finally, is breathed of the possible bequest of an immense National Debt to a generation stripped of the sources of wealth which encouraged and enabled their unscrupulous predecessors to incur it.

The relevant sense, then, in which trade 'follows the flag' is this: that the flag is the means by which the gamblers of trade can best find their way to new grounds of exploitation, leaving the seat of 'empire' at home to sink, it may be, like a deserted ship. Doubtless there is a temporary alternative. Denuded of productive industries, and therefore of industrial population, England may for a time remain a seat of empire as did Italy until the transference of the Roman centre to Constantinople. Her soil would be owned and divided as pleasure-ground among an aristocracy of capitalists, who would employ simply the labour needed for their own service, their incomes being drawn from investments or industries in other regions. With their wealth they might for a time buy army and navy enough for the control of their subject territories, were these menaced, and they might somehow pay or compound for the interest on the National Debt; or they might be spared that outlay by a regimen of peace. But either way, the duration of the empire, as British, would be a mere question of time. No empire can long subsist as such when the sources of its wealth are outside of its proper soil. As we have seen, the one decisive difference of conditions between the British Empire and those of Rome and Spain is the possession of an adequate source of real wealth and power in its home industry. Once that is gone, decadence must follow in the one case as in the others.

It would perhaps not be far wrong to say that commercial decadence is already begun when the cry that 'trade follows the flag' is used to work up the home population to some scheme of 'imperial federation' under which

Imperialism 183

the resources of the colonies may be drawn upon for the forcible expansion and maintenance of empire against rivals. When British trade was in a state of energetic expansion, no such cry was heard. In those days it was taken for granted that in the future, as in the past, trade would naturally go on between different nations, and that Britain was competent to trade with the subjects of other flags, as they with each other. Hundreds of consular reports, however, attest that in recent years British trade is being headed off in many foreign countries by the more intelligent competition of Continental traders, who take pains to meet special demand where the English trader will not. Perhaps, after all, it is sheer prosperity that has made him careless; but there are other possibilities. English life for a generation back has become in every decade more thoroughly leavened with the spirit of gambling; and that spirit normally tends to cast out the methods of scrupulous industry. More and more, for twenty years back, has stock-jobbing enterprise run either to semi-fraudulent domestic undertakings or to foreign mining adventures, which proceed upon no proved knowledge and cater for no sound demand. And so far as is yet seen, the exploitation of South Africa, which is for the present the chief theatre of imperialist instincts and interests, is doing no more for human needs than the gold-mining of the past in California, where one of the permanent results was the destruction of great areas of cultivable land.

In any case, the notion that our trade is to fall back more and more on our colonies and 'possessions' for the future is at once an economic fallacy and a moral retrogression. If it were true that we grow less capable of trading with foreign peoples, it would be a thing to be ashamed of rather than to boast about; and our statesmen, instead of pluming themselves on such a mark of insularity, ought to strive hard to wipe it out. If economic science had not gone so completely out of fashion among them since Cobden's day, they would see that even the competition of other nations with British trade in foreign fields ought in natural course to lead to British gain. Great commercial rivals remain great potential customers. Germany, France, and the United States continue to offer us their special products; and in ordinary course they can be paid for these only by our products. If, then, our statesmen and our traders *believe in the continuance of our productivity* as they affect to do, they should look to increased trade with our rivals themselves as a compensation for their competition with us in outside markets.

But it becomes increasingly doubtful whether our predominant class any longer believes either in a continuance of our productivity or in the scientific principle of Free-trade—the scientific principle, that is, as distinct from the demand that, say, Russia shall not be allowed to secure new ports unless she opens them to our commerce. The suggestion of an imperial federation with a tariff favouring all goods produced within the empire is already a repudiation of the Free-trade principle; and it is, moreover, a resort to a policy which this country refused to permit to China in the past. British trade was forced upon China at the cannon's mouth when her statesmen desired to make a ring-fence round *their* empire. On the new theory, it is our cue to make such a ring-fence for ourselves. And to whose gain? To the gain of capitalists in particular, since the mass of consumers are to pay more for their goods in the name of empire.

Such a policy may please the majority in the mother-country, so completely does the investing and exporting interest at present rule our counsels; but that it can captivate the mass of the colonists is hard to believe. In any event, the resort to it would at once create a capital

186 Patriotism and Empire

difficulty all round, through the forced rivalry of the United States. A differential tariff against the States in Canada would be answered by a worse tariff against Canada in the States; and the existing industrial difficulties of Canada would be made unbearable. Some perception of this appears to be implied in the vague talk about an Anglo-American or 'pan-Anglo-Saxon' alliance, which for the moment has superseded talk about imperial federation. It is a vain dream. In the nature of things there can be no 'pan-Anglo-Saxon alliance,' even if the imperialists of England should grow rational enough to conciliate the hostile Irish element in America and Australia by granting Home Rule to Ireland. The republic and the monarchy cannot join, save for purposes of common-sense diplomacy. The thought of their doing so is but a sentimental outcome of their sinister joint jubilation over the defeat of Spain in the recent American war of aggression. In the lamentably familiar fashion, the spirit of malevolence ministers for the moment to the spirit of union; but never in human history has that ministry meant any durable fraternity. In each State singly, the schism of class interest survives all collusions for national strife; and till that sore is healed, though, haply, there may be abstinence from the supreme stupidity of war, there will be no vital union among separate States. It would be strange indeed if the mass of the people in the colonies should consent to burden themselves with an imperial expenditure for the maintenance of the system which makes life in the mother-country so hard for myriads that they must needs become colonists.

IX

We come back, then, to the vital aspect of imperialism for the mass of the working population. The only interests really furthered by fresh expansion are those of the speculative trading class, the speculative capitalist class, the military and naval services, the industrial class which supplies war material, and generally those who look to an imperial civil service as a means of employment for themselves and their kin. What is more, the present imperialist policy deliberately subsidizes those interests. Parliament has of late years voted huge naval expenditures on the express ground that they are necessary to promote the interests of British commerce. These votes have been granted at times when the unemployed working population was abnormally small. Let, however, the same Parliament be asked to vote a tithe of the sums in question for the relief of masses of unemployed men, and the appeal would be rejected without debate, on the score that such provision is outside the proper functions of Parliament. The proper function of Parliament, as now conceived, is to spend as many millions as possible in the interests of the moneyed and well-to-do minority, while toiling men at the last extremity are left to the niggard operations of the machinery for supporting paupers. The supreme effort bids fair to be made not for the production or diffusion of real wealth, but for the barren enterprise of gold-mining, in the interest of which it is that we are now being embroiled in South Africa, the single one of our ' possessions ' which annually absorbs more wealth than it returns. Such has been the course of imperialism in the past; such will it ever be.

As against all the sophistries we have passed under review, the central truth falls to be stated thus: imperial expansion is substantially a device on the part of the moneyed class, primarily to further its own chances, secondarily to put off the day of reckoning as between capital and labour. It does not and cannot bring a socially just solution any nearer: it does but secure a possible extension of employment for labour on the old terms. In so far, then, as labour is led by any or all of the sophisms of imperialist patriotism, it is gulled to its own ultimate perdition. While imperialism prospers, there will be no vital social reform; and reactionary Ministers have begun to see that by playing the game of militarist imperialism they can safely push aside the appeal for such reform. One of the first sequelæ of the triumph of Omdurman was the definite repudiation of Ministerial promises in the direction of Old Age Pensions. Prestige so won could be set against democratic displeasure. All the while Old Age Pensions, as contemplated from the imperialist point of view, were to be no vital innovation; they were conceived, not as a first step towards the right distribution of wealth and the rectification of industrial evil by maximizing consumption, but rather as a mere dole to mitigate the sordid sorrow of pauperized old age. The Roman Empire did more for its worthless city population of idlers when it gave them bread and games. Yet even this contemplated dole is flinched from when there is reason to think that it can be withheld without party disaster. It is felt to be more important to subsidize the Church and the landlords, as the steadiest backers of the imperialist party.

Under greater pressure, pensions may one day come from the same hands, in the same spirit, for the same end. Meantime it is thought to be sufficient to assure the proletary that he is an heir of empire; that he is one of a dominant race; that he shares in 'our possessions;' that, like Osric in the play, he is 'spacious in the possession of dirt.' If the British proletary be really impressible by such appeals, he is fit for the fate that befalls him— as fit as the Romans who lent themselves to the enslaving of their neighbours at the call of their patrons. But it is the barest justice to him to say that it has never been he who prated of possessions and domination and empire; though some who claim to speak in his name may do so. One finds a professed Socialist candidate for Parliament, one, too, of good standing, reported as telling a meeting of labour-electors that

'He firmly believed in what had been termed the mission of the English peoples. We had a genius for conquest and colonization not possessed, or at least not manifested, by any people of modern times. He believed that it was imperative that we should expand our borders.'

To this pass has it come: the professed champion of the rights of man taking pride in conquest; the professed disciple of economic collectivism playing the game of the land-grabbing capitalist, and declaring that our industrial problem cannot be solved within our own

Imperialism 191

borders, that we must seize other people's territory and exploit them and it. The significance of the position comes out more fully when we remember that the same expansionist formula was put forth by public men in the United States as a special justification for the attack on Cuba. The people of the enormous territory of the Republic, it was averred, needed to expand *their* borders: the margins of profitable enterprise had been reached: they must grab more territory.

If the claim be true—and on the imperialist principle it must be true everywhere sooner or later—the game of democratic civilization, I repeat, is virtually up, and the Socialist is only one more charlatan. If the people of the States cannot win well-being within their present borders they will never win it. Cuba and the Philippines in that aspect are but a passing meal to the Sphinx: to-morrow conclusions must be tried with the Latin republics for South America, or with Russia and England for the richer plains of Asia; and the end in sight is an Armageddon of international piracy. In the name of common-sense and common honesty, come what may, let it at least be told on the housetops, and let who will hear, that the whole doctrine is an insensate superstition, that its economic belongs to the life of the redskins and its sociology to the civilization of Tamerlane.

X

Our imperialistic Socialist, be it noted, is seized by a scruple after he lays down the ethic of expansion, and goes on in a singularly different strain :

'But, nevertheless, he affirmed the necessity of a changed ideal in the prosecution of our territorial ambition and desires. He believed that we should enter upon the comparatively uncivilized portions of the earth not for the purpose of getting so much as of giving. And, furthermore, our gifts should not be, as largely they had been hitherto, the vices and miseries of an outworn civilization, but the benefits and blessings of civilization in its highest and purest sense. (Cheers.)'

The cheers almost suggest that the orator had heard growls at his previous proposition, and was fain to strike instantly a different key. We have a mission for conquest and civilization, but we have displayed it 'largely' by giving to the conquered 'the vices and miseries of an outworn civilization.' How then, in the name of reason, is our outworn civilization in the future to give anything else ? And if we are to cherish our territorial ambitions on the score that it is 'imperative that we should expand our borders,' how, in the name of plausibility, are we to go about the business 'not for the purpose of getting so much as of giving?' Is it the giving that is imperative? Or are we merely getting a lame and impotent Socialist adaptation of the gospel given to the Birmingham jewellers, that it is our mission to 'civilize the tropics,' but for their sake as much as for ours?

To civilize the tropics! With our own race riddled with the leprosy of decivilization, presenting to the eyes that will see, in warren after warren of putrid misery, a life that the zoologist declares to be immeasurably more ignoble than that of the lowest savage whose ways he has scanned! If a fraction of what has been preached in the name of Socialism be true, the conditions of life for millions in England are an infamy, and the whole structure of society is an infinite injustice, whereby the luckless wear their lives out in making wealth for those who neither toil nor spin. And how should such a society yield to any subject society 'the benefits and blessings of civilization in the highest and purest sense'? Is it by turning Japan, the land once of Flowers, into a duplicate of Lancashire, and covering China with the cinder hills and sulphurous reek of the Black Country? Our lyrist of trumpet and drum has hinted at the tropics as a region 'where the best is as the worst.' We are to make it better, it seems, by making Caliban duly subservient to Mammon.

The whole fantasy is a moral imposture. Our Socialist, it is comforting to note, feels the ground giving way beneath his feet :

> 'He would especially give to all such countries the power and opportunity of exercising the powers of local self-government. The manner in which we governed India, for example, in the interests of the Indian officials, and without sufficient regard to the genius and needs of the Indian peoples, formed, in his judgment, one of the gravest national scandals of recent times. In the pursuit of such a policy we were our own worst enemy. Those of our colonies which had received representative institutions at our hands were the most loyal of all our possessions. (Cheers.)'

By this time his imperialism must have an evil odour to the nostrils that dilated over his preamble. He will be told by the 'sane' as well as the other imperialist that he calumniates our Indian rule, and that he knows not whereof he speaks when he talks of giving local government to India. It is indeed hard to guess what part of the empire he had in mind when he grew elate over our mission, if India be ruled as he says. But in his singular five minutes' progress he has reached the answer to the most plausible plea that can ever be framed for empire. No race is really raised, no community is really bettered, while it is held in

Imperialism

subjection, and no man and no class are really raised by putting others below them. The Romans in their day could claim, relatively to their lights, their status and ethic, as much as can the British in theirs; and the Roman imperialist poet could find a rhetoric for the official ideal on which his successors have not improved.

'Pacis imponere morem'

was for him the mission of Rome; and in certain aspects the work was as wonderfully done as anything achieved in modern times. But not one of the protected subjected races was made fit by Roman rule to rule itself. Rome itself was by the process made unfit; and that said, all is said. For if the would-be civilizer does not raise his subjects to worthy manhood, he himself infallibly falls below it. And if, on the other hand, he does so raise them, what becomes of his empire? Let him choose his horn.

Let our devious Socialist take one step more, and he will reach the right lesson for his hearers. The other imperialists have no thought of giving self-government to India; they have scoffed at every step in the movement of the Indian National Congress, and they hate the ends at which it aims. They are exasperated at the suggestion that the Indian Civil Service should be gradually filled with natives; where would be the imperial profit of such an evolution? What of the annihilated English incomes? Rather they will make Anglo-Indian rule yet more imperial, and develop yet further a new imperial caste in the administration of Egypt, and, haply, one day, of China. And then they may hope, not unreasonably, that the irritating pretensions of democracy at home will be with little pains suppressible, and the Radical voter tamed. They may even hope to see the whole system under the due control of an imperator, the surest bar to subversive legislation. Such would be the natural evolution, now as ever. The Socialist who thinks to find in an imperialist and militarist bureaucracy a means to socialistic equity, is by several degrees more optimistic than the Russian Nihilists who thought through the conversion of *their* bureaucracy to carry their ideal.

XI

It becomes irksome to deal further with a pretence of altruism which collapses even in the stating; but it is rather pressingly needful to contrast the pretence squarely with the

Imperialism 197

temper which its framers all the while avow towards their civilized neighbours. We are the friends, it is claimed, of the lower races—at least, of those of them who definitely come under our rule—and when the finger is pointed to the countless infamies of the colonial handling of Maories and Basutos, it is answered that these outrages, uncontrollable where colonists are left a free hand, can best be put down by an imperial system such as now works in India. Considering that the colonists represent the normal attitude of the conqueror towards the lower races, and considering, further, that within a few years we have seen press-gagging laws enforced in India in a way that would not—at least, not yet—be tolerated at home, the claim is sufficiently suspect from the start. But supposing it to pass, to what view of international relations does it lead? In the terms of the case, our first business is to distance the European nations in trade, in power, in prestige. Empire being a good thing for all, we are yet to leave them as little as possible. We are to take satisfaction in their inferiority to us as traders and producers; and it is as sand in our eyes when we see them gaining on us in the race. An imperialist emissary tells gleefully that he has prevented any concessions being made to the French in

China; and his countrymen in council applaud him, trusting that he has helped to keep France poor and to make us rich. As we have seen, an imperialistic economist of the Tamerlane school holds that we are bound to fight Germany one day to the death for the trade of the world; and our pious singer of the White Man's Burden hates the whole Russian race with a frenzy of indecent fury that throws a lurid light on the ethic of his prayers to Deity. What then becomes of the general pretence of imperialistic beneficence? What would be the value, were it genuine, of a sympathy that was tendered to the lower races and the tropic lands on the condition of being compensated for by bitter ill-will and jealousy towards the higher races with whom we have broken bread and shared culture? Of what value to the general deed of man would be a spirit even of protective beneficence towards Hindus on the part of an Anglo-Indian Civil Service that was all the while to be animalized by a savage hatred of Russia as the predestinate enemy?

It is all vain, where it is not vile. The despotism that practises an Egyptian beneficence by way of better extorting the usury on our bonds; the despotism that, after squandering famine funds in lawless frontier wars, rules India with some increase of concern for native good, lest Russia haply intervene—all this is no justification of the theory of empire at its best; and the ingrained duplicity of ideal it involves should be our warning against thinking to endure by it for ever. It seems to be reckoned a marvel by themselves, that Englishmen in the nineteenth century should at last administer better than Orientals of a previous age. It would be their dishonour if they did not; and such modern progress is no vindication of an imperialist ideal in perpetuity. Ideal citizens of a free country are not to be bred by ruling over the unfree, were they thrice picked for character and culture. Some of them may gain many things—the high virtues, it may be, of patience and self-control under provocation, as well as the faculty for various administrative action—but the due wisdom for the life of equality is not to be learned in the life of inequality. The Anglo-Indian who strives and aims to bring the natives under him a little nearer self-rule is indeed doing as high a work as any done on the planet; but not one Anglo-Indian in ten seems to have any such thought. Nor does Anglo-Indian official experience, as a rule, yield us any help toward scientific politics at home. On the other hand, the consciousness that India, with the inconceivable poverty of its masses of cheap life, serves as a pay-chest for thousands of well-nurtured Englishmen, must in itself be sociologically demoralizing, if it does not move the beneficiaries to desire a higher state of things. Such a relation never was and never will be permanently good for any race, ruling or ruled. But the simple biological fact that Englishmen cannot breed in India for two generations might alone serve to convince thinking men that British empire there cannot be permanent, and that a wise policy would consist in preparing for the inevitable change, rather than in defying it. It may or may not have been of the fundamental natural fact that Carlyle was thinking when he told his English hearers that 'India must go one day.' But then Carlyle's context consisted in the proposition that Shakespeare was for English-speaking men a greater possession than India; and as this would at once mark him a Little Englander in the eyes of the large-thoughted school of Osric, whose Shakespeare is Mr. Kipling, it is by that sage formula disposed of.

This megalomania, which regards relative smallness of territory as a ground for contempt, gives a new clue to that hatred for Russia of which Mr. Kipling is the foremost propagator. Our imperialist Russophobes must be gnawed hourly by the worst of pangs, when they reflect that Russian territory in Europe and Asia outbulks British; and the thought that little Scandinavia can be made great by literature must appear to them as preposterous as the opinion that little Athens availed more for human enlightenment than imperial Rome. There is no use in arguing with the snob, whether he be the snob national or the snob social; and it is visibly a mere adaptation of the snob's code that yields us the Big Englander. But it is necessary to point out what he is bringing us to. Of Bismarck, as before noted, it has been said that he made Germany great, but made small the German. But it does not need a Bismarck to do that for any nation, as regards the latter half of the process at least. It only needs that its members should count it a littleness to seek greatness within rather than without, and should believe it possible to make themselves great Englanders by making an externally great England. Accept for a generation the ideal of those who hold a nation great in the measure of its acreage, and who scout the idea that a small country can be worth belonging to, and you *will* have a country not worth belonging to for two-thirds of its people. We always come back to that.

XII

Our indictment is now outlined and argued; and it is not at the end of an indictment that a counter-ideal is best to be set forth. But lest it be supposed that the counter-ideal is not capable of clear definition, that may be curtly outlined in contrast.

As thus: Against a policy of racial swagger, external force, expansion, gold-mining, and other exploitation of filched territory, a policy of scientific social development, to the end of a maximization of real wealth and a better distribution thereof.

As against an ever-increasing expenditure on naval armaments, which merely forces to similar and countervailing expenditure the neighbour States who feel themselves menaced by it, expenditure in bettering the lives of our wealth-makers, and in educating their children for further betterment.

As against a mechanical concept of union, involving eternal ill-will to England from Irishmen throughout the world, an intelligent federation of the sections of the Mother State, with Home Rule to all who need it.

As against the Roman ideal of perpetual domination in India and Egypt, the ideal of a loyal development of their peoples, however slowly so it be surely, towards freedom and self-government.

As against a perpetual overbreeding which drives out yearly an army of exiles, a rational control of population in all classes.

As against a shiftless drift towards the headlong downfall of empire and population when our coal-supply is exhausted, a rational construction of alternate bases for a sounder civilization, whose fruits may haply be beauty and not ashes.

And lastly, as against a barbarian cult, which alternately chants a hypocritical hymn of propitiation to a God of War and bares venomous fangs towards the rival worshippers of the same deity, an ethic of reason and fraternity, of human goodwill, that guards against supernaturalist vitiations.

In fine, wisdom and righteousness for a nation are not vitally different from what we esteem as wisdom and righteousness in individual men. And that nation which thinks to prosper by inverting the principles of stable human relation, by calling rapine righteousness and profligacy prudence, will but illustrate sooner or later the fatality of natural law. On such lines no nation as such can survive. . The conclusion is not one of a too ideal ethic: it is the lesson read to us in age after age, in civilization after civilization, by empire after empire that has left only its ruins behind to warn us against the errors by which it perished.

ADDENDA

Note to pages 100-103.

SINCE these pages were written there has appeared a second edition of Captain Mahan's *Life of Nelson*, in which the case against the hero is more fully dealt with by his biographer, the Italian evidence being now taken up. The revised vindication is, however, rebutted afresh by Mr. Badham in the *Athenæum* of July 1, 1899. Captain Mahan replies in the same journal, July 8, to small purpose.

Note to page 109.

I am reminded that 'Algeria, in the early times of the French occupation, saw arise, every spring, fanatics who declared themselves invulnerable and sent by God to drive out the infidels; next year their death was forgotten, and their successors found no less faith' (Renan, *Vie de Jésus*, chap. iv.). The completest obliteration of any one Mahdi is thus no hindrance to others following in his steps, and the Soudan episode is thus doubly gratuitous in the light of French experience in Algeria.

Note to page 184.

In regard to the proposition that 'trade follows the flag,' it is worth noting that British trade with the Argentine Republic is greater than British trade proper with all the colonies of South and East Africa; and is besides profitable, whereas that is not. In 1896 our imports from South and East Africa were under five and a half millions, while our exports thither were over fourteen millions. To the Argentine Republic, in the same year, we exported over six and a half millions, importing nearly nine millions. With variations of quantity, these proportions generally hold.

INDEX

Africa, South, 183, 184, 205
Alberoni, 164
Alexander, 131
Alfred, 97
Anglo-Saxonism, 62, 186
Arnold, 39
Athens, 92, 93, 146-150

Badham, F. P., 101, 102, 205
Bellamy, 48
Beneficence, imperialist, 192-200
Bismarck, 22-28, 57, 59, 107, 113
Byzantium, 95

Cæsar, 87, 97, 130, 131
Canada, 169
Carlyle, 200
Chatham, Lord, 163-167
China, 90, 143, 144, 175, 180, 185, 193
Class subsidies, 187-189
Coal-supply, 172, 180
Coleridge, 13, 18
Colonial justice, 197
Consciousness of kind, 5
Conway, Dr. M., 49
Cook, Captain E., 124, 125
Cox, Sir G., 2
Crimean War, 76
Cromwell, 87, 97, 131, 161, 163
Cuban War, 7, 8, 61, 126, 136, 186, 191

Dante, 63
Debt, National, 166, 168, 181, 182
Delafosse, 86, 87
Dickens, 47, 49

Disarmament, 134-136
Disraeli, 55, 139, 140, 142
Dreyfus case, 104, 106-108

Eastwick, Captain, 124, 125
Economics, 56, 167, 174-188
Egyptian civilization, 92
Emerson, 44
Emigration, 174-177
Empires, ancient, 95
English history, 13-21, 88, 158, 159, 161
Epaminondas, 120, 121
Expansionism, 52, 173-182, 191

Flag, trade and, 174, 205
Fleury, 164
Florence, 151, 158
Fox, 14
Frederick, 97, 121, 131
Free-trade, 185
French culture, 113
  history, 161, 165, 166, 169, 171
  militarism, 106-108, 110
  resources, 181
  Revolution, 13-18

German developments, 22-28, 57, 107, 111-116, 177
Germany and England, 56-59
Gladstone, 55, 139-142
Gracchi, the, 156, 157
Grant, 98, 131
Greek history, 2, 89, 119, 146-150
Grote, 2, 120 n.

Hamon, 104

Index

Hannibal, 96, 156
Hawthorne, 64
Henley, 52-55, 59, 62
Higginson, Colonel, 39-43
Highland clearances, 21
Homer, 63, 64
Hugo, 40
Huysmans, 49

Imperialism, 138-204
India, 144, 170, 180, 194-200
Irish nationalism, 28-30, 186, 202
Irving, Washington, 47
Italy, 28, 29, 177

Jackson, 98
'Jago,' the, 31-37
Japan, 180, 193
Johnson, Dr., 41
Jones, Paul, 103

Kipling, 52-55, 60, 161, 193, 198, 200
Kitchener, 53, 109

Lee, 131
Leopardi, 64
Lincoln, 98
Literature and patriotism, 63
'Little England,' 161, 168
Lowell, 45, 46, 62, 63

Macaulay, 41, 170
Machiavelli, 64, 96, 158
Mahan, 83-91, 94, 100 n., 110, 205
Mahdism, 109, 205
Marius, 95
Marlborough, 131
Marx, 48
Megalomania, 200, 201
Militarism, 71-137
Moltke, 57, 113, 131
Mommsen, 112, 113
Moors, 151
Morris, 48
Motley, 47, 48

Napoleon, 97, 121, 126, 131
Natural enemies, 36
Nelson, 99-103, 131, 205
Newcome, Colonel, 105
Nietzsche, 113

Nihilism, 197
Nile, Battle of the, 125, 126

Old-age pensions, 189
Opportunism, 55
Osric, ideal of, 190, 200

Palmerston, 142
Patriotism, 1-70, 155, 156, 161
Peloponnesian War, 89, 93, 146
Pericles, 12, 148
Poe, 44
Population question, 176, 203
Poverty, English, 179

Ram, J., 82, n.
Religion, militarist, 132, 198, 203
Rhodes, Mr., 53
Roman history, 8-10, 147, 150, 151-157, 162, 182, 189, 195
Rostand, 3-5
Russian culture, 113
Ryan, Dr. C. E., 132

Savonarola, 158
Scandinavian life, 113
Sedan, Battle of, 129, 130
Sentimentalism, 81
Shakespeare, 63, 64, 119, 200
Skirving, 15-18
Social problem, 9, 19, 48, 61, 78, 86, 91, 172, 173, 178-182, 187, 188, 193, 202, 203
Socialism, 48, 84, 136, 190, 193
Socrates, 150
Spain, 151, 159-164, 181 182
Sparta, 1, 2, 10, 11, 92, 93, 121, 147
Stephen, L., 41
Sulla, 95
Suttner, Baroness, 133
Swiss history, 12

Tennyson, 170
Thackeray, 128, 129
Thermopylæ, 1, 2, 5, 10
Thirlwall, 2
Thucydides, 93
Timoleon, 97
Trade, English, 183
Turkey, 116, 117

Unionism, 141
United States, 7, 8, 39-51, 58, 60-64, 89, 126, 127, 136, 175, 177

Verestchagin, 127

Walpole, 163-166

War, 118
Washington, 98, 131
Wellington, 98-100, 131
Whitman, 44

Zola, 128, 129

THE END.

BILLING AND SONS, PRINTERS, GUILDFORD.

www.ingramcontent.com/pod-product-compliance
Lightning Source LLC
Chambersburg PA
CBHW031815220426
43662CB00007B/657